The Last Interview

Primo Levi

The Last Interview
Conversations with
Giovanni Tesio

Translated and with an introduction by
Judith Woolf

polity

First published in Italian as *Io che vi parlo. Conversazione con Giovanni Tesio* © Giulio Einaudi editore s.p.a, Turin, 2016

This English edition © Polity Press, 2018

Polity Press
65 Bridge Street
Cambridge CB2 1UR, UK

Polity Press
101 Station Landing
Suite 300
Medford, MA 02155, USA

ISBN-13: 978-1-5095-1954-5
ISBN-13: 978-1-5095-1955-2 (pb)

A catalogue record for this book is available from the British Library.

Library of Congress Cataloging-in-Publication Data

Names: Levi, Primo, author. | Tesio, Giovanni, 1946- interviewer.
Title: The last interview : conversation with Giovanni Tesio / Primo Levi.
Other titles: Lo che vi parlo. English
Description: Medford, MA : Polity, [2018] | Includes bibliographical references and index.
Identifiers: LCCN 2017058561 (print) | LCCN 2017059366 (ebook) | ISBN 9781509519583 (Epub) | ISBN 9781509519545 (hardback) | ISBN 9781509519552 (pbk.)
Subjects: LCSH: Levi, Primo–Interviews. | Authors, Italian–20th century–Interviews. | Jewish authors–Italy–Interviews. | Holocaust survivors–Italy–Interviews.
Classification: LCC PQ4872.E8 (ebook) | LCC PQ4872.E8 Z4613 2018 (print) | DDC 858/.91409–dc23
LC record available at https://lccn.loc.gov/2017058561

Typeset in 11 on 14 pt Sabon by Toppan Best-set Premedia Limited
Printed and bound in Great Britain by Clays Ltd, Elcograf S.p.A.

For further information on Polity, visit our website: politybooks.com

Contents

Introduction

The conversations in this book were intended as material for an authorized biography, but they were also an act of kindness. The literary critic Giovanni Tesio had realized that his friend Primo Levi was suffering from severe depression which left him feeling unable to write, and thought that working together in this way might be consoling and even therapeutic. Consequently these transcriptions are in one sense an intimate record of life events shared with a friend, but in another and very important sense they enable us to overhear the words of a very reserved and private man who paradoxically used his own experiences as the basis for his greatest work.

There are good reasons for Levi's desire to keep his home life out of the public sphere. Turin, his native city, was proverbially reserved and respectful of the proprieties, and his upbringing there was a typically bourgeois one. For a young man from such a background, one of the most devastating aspects of the barbarities he suffered in Auschwitz was that, along with their clothes and their hair and even their names, prisoners were stripped of every last shred of privacy, a degrading and depersonalizing process which began in the cattle trucks, devoid of so much as a bucket, in which deportees were transported to brief slavery or immediate death. The impulse, as he shouldered the life-long task of bearing witness, to close the front door of 75 Corso Re Umberto on a protected space, must have been overwhelming. In addition, his growing international renown, which reached its peak with the English translation, in 1984, of *The Periodic Table*, meant that he came to be seen, much against his will, as some kind of guru or secular saint, whose Holocaust accounts were thought to represent not a grim and needed warning but a triumph of the human spirit. As he told Tesio, he felt 'gradually overwhelmed, first in Italy and then abroad, by this wave of success which has profoundly affected my equilibrium and put me in the shoes of someone I am not'. From this, too, the private space with which he was able to surround himself at his writing desk, as he had earlier done at his laboratory bench in the Siva paint and varnish factory, offered a much-needed retreat.

While it was Auschwitz, from which he returned 'like Coleridge's Ancient Mariner, who waylays on the street the wedding guests going to the feast, inflicting on them the story of his misfortune',[1] which first compelled him to write about what he had suffered, observed and, exceptionally, survived, Levi was also to become a witness of a very different kind, attempting with considerable success to bridge the needless gulf which separates the so-called two cultures with dispatches from the world of pure and applied chemistry. This book should be read alongside

---

[1]Primo Levi, *The Periodic Table*, trans. Raymond Rosenthal, London: Michael Joseph, 1985, p. 151. All notes in the text are the translator's, unless marked GT (Giovanni Tesio).

The Periodic Table, to which it adds valuable background material about his schooldays and his emotional life as a young man, but to understand why sharing the pleasures and pains of a chemist's trade was so important to Levi, it is necessary to go into a little detail about the educational system in Italy during the Fascist period.

It is well known that Levi narrowly escaped being excluded from a university education by the passing of the anti-Semitic racial laws, and was prevented by them from going on to the academic career which, as a student who had graduated with top marks and distinction, would otherwise have been open to him. However, the frustration he felt as a schoolboy, with the narrowly arts-based curriculum which forced him to discover science through his own reading and his experiments with household chemicals, was also due to Fascist policy. As Martin Clark explains, 'the Fascists inherited a "three-stream" system of secondary education: the *ginnasio* and *liceo* [lower and higher secondary schools] for the social élite, the technical schools and technical institutes for the commercial middle classes, and the *scuole normali* for girls wanting to become primary teachers ... The Fascists soon changed all that. In 1923, Giovanni Gentile, as minister of education, reorganized secondary education.' Under these reforms, initiated as they were by an idealist philosopher, the old technical schools were abolished and 'access to, and the status of, the technical institutes was greatly reduced, as was admission to the university science faculties'. One curious effect of this reorganization was that 'Latin, Italian, History and Philosophy were taught by men, whereas Mathematics, Physics and Chemistry continued to be taught by women. This was an apt comment on Fascist male chauvinism', and it is an apt comment too on how the subjects which mattered most to Levi were now regarded. Another effect was that 'Italy produced fewer engineers, scientists and

doctors in the late 1930s than the early 1920s.'[2] Access to
higher education was now largely dependent on attending
a *liceo classico* such as the Massimo D'Azeglio school,
where Levi endured rather than enjoyed a syllabus based
on those prestige subjects, turning him into a passionate
advocate for the integrated culture which was shared by
'Empedocles, Dante, Leonardo, Galileo, Descartes, Goethe
and Einstein, the anonymous builders of the Gothic cathe-
drals and Michelangelo' and is still shared by 'the good
craftsmen of today, or the physicists hesitating on the brink
of the unknowable'.[3]

However, the most significant and moving revelation in
The Last Interview does not concern either education or
chemistry. Although Tesio suggests in his preface, 'I knew
Primo Levi', that 'the real difference in our conversations,
as compared with other interviews, was more in the tone
than the content', in one painful respect Levi confided
something to him which stitches together the repeated but
oblique references throughout his writing to a 'woman
who was dear to my heart' who had been deported to
Auschwitz with him.[4] That woman was Vanda Maestro, a
close friend and fellow partisan, and Levi reveals to Tesio
that he had been in love with her but had felt too shy and
inhibited fully to reveal his feelings. He had returned from
Auschwitz already knowing how she had died: 'her name
pronounced among those of the condemned, her descent
from the bunk of the infirmary, her setting off (in full con-
sciousness!) towards the gas chamber and the cremation

---

[2]Martin Clark, *Modern Italy: 1871–1995*, London and New York:
Longman, 1996, pp. 276–7.
[3]Primo Levi, *Other People's Trades*, trans. Raymond Rosenthal,
London: Michael Joseph, 1989, p. viii.
[4]*The Periodic Table*, op. cit., p. 151.

oven',[5] and was tormented by the irrational but inevitable feeling that if only he had acted differently perhaps he and she might have been elsewhere when their partisan band was rounded up. 'It was a really desperate situation for me, being in love with someone who was gone and, what's more, whose death one had caused, and I think that what one feels is … Perhaps if I had been less inhibited with her, if we had run away together, if we had made love … I was incapable of those things.'

Tesio at one point suggests to Levi that his writing is characterized by 'a sort of holding back', and Levi himself, when asked why he has written so little about the Fossoli internment camp, repeats three times, '*ho delle remore*' [I have qualms], adding 'And also about that woman I told you of'. A *remora* is a qualm, a hesitation, a scruple, an impediment, but Levi would have known that it is also the name of a family of fish, the Echeneidae or suckerfish, which in classical mythology were believed to be able to hold back any ship they attached themselves to. All this adds an extra poignancy to Levi's poem 'Il tramonto di Fossoli' [Sunset at Fossoli],[6] dated 7 February 1946, in which he translates the famous lines from Catullus's Poem V:

> soles occidere et redire possunt;
> nobis cum semel occidit brevis lux,

---

[5]'Testimony for a fellow prisoner', in Primo Levi and Leonardo De Benedetti, *Auschwitz Testimonies: 1945–1986*, trans. Judith Woolf, Cambridge: Polity Press, 2017, p. 64. This is the concluding passage of a moving tribute to Vanda Maestro, originally published anonymously in a book in memory of Piedmontese women partisans, *Donne piemontesi nella lotta di liberazione* [Piedmontese Women in the Struggle for Liberation], printed in 1953.
[6]Primo Levi, *Collected Poems*, trans. Ruth Feldman and Brian Swann, London: Faber, 1992, p. 15.

nox est perpetua una dormienda.
[suns can set and rise again;
but we, when our brief light has set,
will have an endless night to sleep.]

The rest of Catullus's poem urges living and loving, and
the exchange of countless kisses, as the best antidote to the
fear of death, but Levi describes remembering these lines
as he looks at the sunset through the barbed wire of the
internment camp and feeling them lacerate his flesh. As in
The Periodic Table, he also tells Tesio of the euphoria of
falling instantly in love with his future wife, a life-changing
encounter, celebrated in a poem written only four days
after 'Sunset at Fossoli' and titled '11 February 1946',[7]
which 'exorcized the name and face of the woman who
had gone down into the lower depths with me and had
not returned',[8] but Vanda is constantly in his mind as he
talks about his early life.

The Italian title of this book, *Io che vi parlo*, literally means 'I who am speaking to you', neatly, if rather
untranslatably, putting the emphasis on the first person
and the speaking voice. Polity Press has chosen instead
to give the English edition a title which not only reflects
the fact that Levi's conversations with Tesio were among
the final interviews which he gave at the end of his life,
but also hauntingly underlines what the final sentence of
Tesio's preface makes movingly clear. Levi's last interview
was the one which didn't happen: he was just about to
'resume the work' of telling Tesio his life story when his
life came to its sudden and tragic end. This does not mean
that these conversations should be scrutinized for clues
or premonitions, not least because the true circumstances

[7]*Collected Poems*, op. cit., p. 16.
[8]*The Periodic Table*, op. cit., p. 153.

of Levi's death will never be known: there is no witness and no suicide note to tell us whether it was caused by a momentary blackout as he leaned over the banisters or the different blackness of a moment of overwhelming despair, and perhaps we should cease to speculate and leave him that final privacy. Although critics and biographers all too often try to shape their narratives by beginning Levi's story at its end, the manner of his death does not give us the measure of the man, or of a lifetime spent in the service both of chemistry, which as he told Tesio he saw as fundamental to everything from 'the starry sky' to the smallest gnat, and of human liberty, which he defended to the limits of his strength on behalf of us all.

Judith Woolf

I knew Primo Levi

Creating a space for conversation requires the efforts of
an alpinist.

Osip Mandelštam, *Conversation about Dante*

'Do you already have a plan of attack in mind?' I was
asked this question in the study of an apartment on the
third floor of 75 Corso Re Umberto – one of the most
elegant streets in Turin – on the afternoon of 12 January
1987.

Asking it was one of the most pacific writers to have
crossed, not only in a literary sense, our twentieth-
century stage, one of the most authoritative witnesses
to Auschwitz, a man of undoubted integrity but just
as undoubtedly wounded in spirit and flesh: a master
of secularism and reason, of doubt and questioning, but also of clarity and resistance, of resolve and
action.

In the austerely spacious study, in that house which
resembled 'many other quasi-patrician houses of the turn
of the century' (as he wrote in an account later published

in *Other People's Trades*),[9] Primo Levi asked me that entirely predictable question, which nonetheless disconcerted me. But to account both for the predictability of the question and for my astonishment at hearing it put to me, I need to give some preliminary explanation.

I first encountered Primo Levi by reading *If This is a Man* in the Einaudi 'Corallo' edition in 1967. And ten years later I got to know him in person, because leafing through a school anthology devoted to Piedmontese writers,[10] I discovered that the pages chosen by the editor did not correspond in the least with my enduring memory of the text of *If This is a Man* in the edition I had read. Having compared them, I was able to discover that there existed a text previous to the Einaudi edition, and that this text had been published in 1947 by the De Silva publishing house which Franco Antonicelli, one of the leading figures in Turinese anti-fascism, had founded in '42 and which had closed down in '49. Comparing the De Silva text with the first Einaudi edition of 1958, which has remained identical in subsequent reprintings, I then discovered that the variants were neither few nor insignificant. So I plucked up my courage (in Piedmontese there is a fine saying, to put on a '*bon bèch*', which literally means a 'good beak') and telephoned the author, who without hesitation invited me to his house and put at my disposal an exercise book: a thick school exercise book with an olive green cover, in which I was able to check the text of the parts which had been added. And so I wrote an article,[11] in truth rather

[9]Primo Levi, *Other People's Trades*, trans. Raymond Rosenthal, London: Michael Joseph, 1989, p. 1.
[10]*Il cuore e il sangue della terra* [The Heart and Blood of the Land], ed. Virginia Galante Garrone, 1976. (GT)
[11]'Su alcune giunte e varianti di *Se questo è un uomo*' [On some additions and variants in *If This is a Man*], in *Studi Piemontesi*, VI, 1977, n. 2. (GT)

hybrid and certainly not perfect (I did not take account of the chapters already published thanks to Silvio Ortona in the Vercellese Communist journal *L'Amico del Popolo* [The Friend of the People]), but which all the same had a modest success.

After this, I returned to question Levi again about the problem of variants. And it was he who allowed me to look not only at the handwritten exercise book in which he had composed nearly all the chapters of *The Truce*, but – in due course – at the typescript of *The Wrench* prepared for publication, which took place in '78. So I could be quite sure that he was referring to me when, with the arrival of the computer, he wrote an article called 'The Scribe' for *La Stampa* (later collected in *Other People's Trades*), in which he talks about a 'literary friend' who laments the loss of 'the noble joy of the philologist intent on reconstructing, through successive erasures and corrections, the itinerary which leads to the perfection of the *Infinite*'.[12]

After that first piece of work, others followed. First of all a 'critical portrait' published in *Belfagor*[13] two years later. And then quite a number of reviews and interviews. So that when he was thinking of publishing the poems of *Ad Ora Incerta* [At an Uncertain Hour], he consulted me – it was the time when Einaudi was going through its most acute crisis, which saw the diaspora of other writers, for example Lalla Romano, who published *Nei mari estremi* [The Furthest Seas] with Mondadori – about

---

[12]*Other People's Trades*, op. cit., p. 79. The passage that Tesio quotes refers specifically to Giacomo Leopardi's 1819 poem, *L'infinito*, but omitting Leopardi's name gives the poem's title a universal significance here.
[13]*Belfagor*, founded by Luigi Russo in 1946, was a distinguished Italian scholarly journal of the humanities. It ceased publication in 2012.

finding another possible and worthy publisher, and I suggested that he should consider Garzanti, as in fact he did.

Levi was unassuming, sober, discreet and very courteous. And I was fascinated not only by the expressive precision of his books, by his wide-ranging and detailed knowledge, by his remarkable memory, but also by his receptiveness and his undoubted and special ability to communicate with precise and succinct words, in which all the same there vibrated a note which was not without some trace of melancholy: that ability of his to avoid all superfluities and to base his writing instead on a rich and ornate sobriety of language, on the plain elegance of the *mot-chose*.

To have got to know Levi also means this: recognizing in his written words the grain of his speaking voice: anti-rhetorical but not inert, familiar but almost festive, a monotone which was capable of expressive power.

There grew up between us something that was more than mere civility. So much so as to permit us to address each other as *tu* rather than *lei*[14] and to justify the more than commonplace dedications in the books which he sent me from time to time. In short, a certain familiarity had established itself between us and a combination of circumstances led to the idea of these conversations, which I proposed to Levi at a time when I thought they might help him. I did not have a clear plan to begin with, but I was certainly applying a precept often tested and repeatedly confirmed by Levi, that 'talking is the best medicine'.[15]

In his *Conversations with Primo Levi*, Ferdinando Camon at a certain point, perhaps with reference to personal

---

[14]Moving from the formal to the informal Italian pronoun when addressing someone as 'you' has a similar significance to being on first name terms in the English-speaking world.

[15]Primo Levi, 'The Molecule's Defiance' in *Lilith and Other Stories*, trans. Ann Goldstein, *The Complete Works of Primo Levi*, Vol. II, London: Penguin Random House, 2015, p. 1507.

experiences later converted into fiction, says to Levi, 'You're not a depressed man, and not even anxious'. And the writer, obviously curious about this unexpected remark, replies with a question, 'Is that a feeling you get from my books or from my presence?' To which Camon replies in his turn, 'From your presence', eliciting this clarification:

> In general, you're right. Since the concentration camp, however, I've had a few attacks of depression. I'm not sure if they go back to that experience, because they come with different labels, from one to the next. It may seem strange to you, but I went through one just recently, a stupid fit of depression, for very little reason: I had a small operation on my foot, and this made me think that I'd suddenly got old. It took two months for the wound to heal. That's why I asked you if the feeling came from my presence or my books.[16]

The interview with Camon was the result of a number of meetings which took place between '82 and '86 (the last, on a Sunday at the end of May '86, less than a year before his death). And given that it is an interview which has been ordered by themes, it is hard to say whether the statement I have just quoted belongs to the final meeting. Presumably yes, but it is not clear.

However that may be, on Christmas Eve '86 I proposed to Levi that we should put together the material for a biography which from the start we were calling 'authorized'. I had unexpectedly become aware of his breakdown and, I don't know why, the impulse came to me to suggest to him a project which, to be honest, I had not even vaguely

[16]Ferdinando Camon, *Conversations with Primo Levi*, trans. John Shepley, Marlboro, VT: The Marlboro Press, 1989, p. 63. Camon's book was originally published under the title *Autoritratto di Primo Levi* [Self-Portrait of Primo Levi].

thought about until that moment. That was how I instinctively adopted the expedient of an 'authorized biography'. And he accepted it right away, to my surprise, without making any objections.

That was why I went to his house on the afternoon of 12 January in the New Year, 1987, taking with me a little tape-recorder. And there it all began with the words, 'Do you already have a plan of attack in mind?' And I was forced to admit that I did not have a plan in mind at all – let alone a 'plan of attack' – and I certainly had not prepared, as Camon specifies that he had done for his interview, 'a systematic set of questions, issues, and problems, making sure that they were related to [his] entire life and work'.[17] Instead, I aimed, for the moment, at gathering the greatest possible quantity of information and data. We did not establish any rules or procedures apart from conversing in mainly chronological order, with an eye, for the time being, more on events and people than on issues: simple directions for a journey which would discover its own best route as it went along.

After that first meeting, on 12 January 1987, there were two others, both in the afternoon, one on 26 January and the other on 8 February. I more than once turned off the tape-recorder to allow him to speak more freely about things which he was reluctant to have recorded: sometimes he asked me to do this, on other occasions I used my own initiative. Apart from that, our agreement was clear. At one particular juncture in our conversations it was Levi himself who reminded me that his confessions would have to be 'translated'. He said this to me at a moment when he explicitly acknowledged that he was 'in crisis': 'I've told you from the start that these are confessions which will need to be translated', or rather, to be interpreted.

---

[17]Camon, op. cit., p. 2.

The real difference in our conversations, as compared with other interviews, was more in the tone than the content: the timbre, the gesture. While his words were no less precise than usual, his bearing sometimes showed signs of weakness. So much so that after the second of our meetings – contrary to our usual custom, which did not extend beyond a firm handshake – at the moment of leave-taking he embraced me.

After our third meeting he told me that we would have to take a break because he was going into hospital for an operation. He forbade me as he knew how, with a gentle firmness which did not allow any insistence, either to come and visit him in the clinic or to phone his family to ask for news. And I followed his instructions.

Before his operation I went to his house one more time in order to take him an anthology of mine, which had just been published, in which I had chosen the story 'Arsenic' from *The Periodic Table*: he did not seem displeased and told me that the story had recently been translated into Chinese. I found him with Alberto Salmoni, the real Emilio of *The Periodic Table*. But it was a very brief visit which all took place in the doorway of his house.

When I decided to get in touch with him again it was already April. On Good Friday, at about noon, I called him on the telephone. He answered it himself and his voice was very friendly and not without good humour. Before I could ask, he announced that he was ready to 'resume the work'. Only he warned me to avoid that Sunday, because an 'American photographer' was coming for a feature and he would have to entertain her. And so it was agreed that I should call him back the following week to make that appointment which we were never able to keep.

Giovanni Tesio

Acknowledgements

Grateful thanks are due to Maurizio Crosetti and Guido Davico Bonino for their reading of this book, and to Fabio Levi for his role as intermediary and sponsor.

Monday, 12 January

Do you already have a plan of attack in mind?

I'd like to proceed in chronological order, starting with memories of your parents, of your father and mother, and where they came from. In short, I'd like to trace a picture of your family, your grandparents on both sides ... Shall we begin with your father?

You already know many things about my father from *The Periodic Table*, and I can add a few more. He died prematurely at the age of sixty-four from a tumour. While he was still in good health, he was a man who knew how to enjoy life. He had a great thirst for knowledge and learning. He had travelled a good deal and spoke fluent French and German. When he was sixty he started learning English, and relearning integral calculus. He had already studied it as an engineer, but he used to practise it. I still sometimes find notes of his in the house, especially exercises in integral calculus, solved and unsolved.

Where did he travel?

He travelled first of all to France and Belgium, and later he spent a few years in Hungary, in Budapest.

Always for some firm?

Yes. During the First World War he was in Italy, but he was exempt from military service because he was running a ball bearing factory which was of use to the war effort. So he was considered to be indispensable.

Where was the factory?

As far as I remember, in Turin, but I don't know which factory it was. He was caught in Budapest by the First World War, but those were different times and instead of putting him in a concentration camp they sent him back to Italy with a travel permit and he arrived safe and sound. Later he kept up his connection with Hungary. He worked for a large mechanical and electrical construction company and was the project manager there. Later on, after I and my sister were born, he became the representative for this company in Piedmont and Liguria. He almost gave up being an engineer, in the strict sense of the word, but as representative it was he who supervised the assembly of this equipment, so he travelled through the whole of Piedmont and Liguria.

A very energetic man.

He was a voracious man, in both senses of the word: voracious, because he was eager to find out a bit about everything, he used to read a great deal, and voracious, because he was a *bon viveur*, he was very fond of eating good food. He never became what you would call wealthy. Every now and then I think there was talk at home about buying a car, but having a car was still a fantasy in those days, and one was never bought.

You were a well-to-do family.

Yes, we were fairly well off, reasonably well off. We had a live-in maid, but in those days it was quite common to have a live-in maid. She did everything, she was devoted to Saint Rita and made cautious attempts to convert us to Catholicism. She was obliging and very calm.

Shall we go back to your father?

My father was well known for various anecdotes, for his jackets, for his books, and because he checked the price of ham with a slide rule. The pork butcher in Cogne,[1] who had seen him rapidly checking and multiplying in an instant, bought himself one in Aosta and then complained to my father, 'But mine doesn't work!' It's not that easy. These days it's like an archaeological find, nobody has one any more, it's something which dates back forty years. These days it's an antique instrument. I still have the one which belonged to my father.

As an heirloom?

If you need to do a rough multiplication in a hurry, it's faster than an electronic calculator.

---

[1] Cogne, a town in the Aosta Valley 140 kilometres from Turin, was one of the places where the Levi family spent country summer holidays.

What was your father like physically?

Quite short and heavily built, very sturdy. He boasted of never having gone to the dentist in his life. He had never taken part in any kind of sport, but all the same he had a striking natural physical presence, he was a man with a strong constitution.

While we are on the subject of your father, it seems to me that you didn't have a Jewish upbringing.

Yes and no. My father was very conflicted, even though he wouldn't have said so. He had boarded with a rabbi and had absorbed a certain amount. But he had absorbed the ritual more than anything else. He had scruples about eating ham, but he ate it all the same. I remember that he took me to the synagogue a few times, at Yom Kippur. He would fast in the sense that he skipped breakfast, but then he would eat lunch, so essentially, when it came to religion in the serious sense of the word, I would say that more than anything he was anti-traditional. Even at the level of conversation, he didn't really talk about it. I remember him saying to me, when I must have been four years old, 'We are Jews'. I asked him what that meant and he made a speech that I didn't understand and I connected the word for Jews: *ebrei* with the word for books: *libri*, and there still exists for me a falsely etymological relationship between *libro* and *ebreo*. I would stress, falsely etymological.

There is an assonance though …

It's an assonance which is not without significance, because the Jews are the people of the book. These are all things that I wasn't aware of then, perhaps not even my father was aware of them. Certainly he never urged me to make it obvious at school that I was Jewish. My parents and my schoolmistress both warned me about this. At that time in elementary school everyone had to stand up at the start of lessons and say the Pater Noster, and I used to stand up though I didn't say the Pater Noster. I remember a caress from my teacher who appreciated this sign of respect for the majority religion. And when there was a religious studies lesson, I and a Waldensian[2] were asked to leave and we had to spend a boring hour on a bench in the corridor waiting for the lesson to finish.

Did you simply experience all this as boredom, or did you also have the feeling that it was discrimination?

Just as boredom, not discrimination.

Did you have a normal relationship with your classmates at elementary school?

At elementary school it was completely normal.

While later, on the other hand ...

I ought to begin by saying that Judaism as a religion was not passed on to me; Judaism as a way of life, to a certain extent, yes, because it is likely that my father's indiscriminate ability to read and to learn was a Jewish inheritance, it was shared with his two brothers, both very different from him, but all three of them used to steal books from

---

[2] The Waldensians, a pre-Protestant sect founded in the twelfth century by Peter Waldo, joined the wider Protestant movement at the Reformation, but still maintained their own religious identity in Piedmont.

each other, they would let each other know when an interesting book came out, they read French. My father read German as well, he took it into his head to read Schopenhauer in the original German, without understanding very much of it, he didn't have the background. He had been to a technical school, not a *liceo*,[3] so he wasn't able to understand very much of it.

But he still wanted to.

He was certainly very eager to. I remember that, because he was also a bit of a ladies' man.

A bon viveur *in all senses.*

Yes, he would try to seduce my mother's women friends by telling them about Schopenhauer, without much success. They used to laugh at him a little behind his back, they thought he was a bit of a madman. He made a discovery: do you remember *Il giornalino di Gian Burrasco* by Vamba?[4] It was plagiarized. It's odd that no one has noticed this, because before *Il giornalino di Gian Burrasco* was published, my father read us, in Italian, its German counterpart. There was a book, I don't remember the title, I only remember a few words: it was the story of a naughty little boy, but it was almost literally the same as

[3] *Liceo* [senior high school], the final three years of secondary education, was preceded by five years of *ginnasio* [junior high school]. For an account of the Italian school system during the Fascist period, see *Introduction*, pp. viii–ix.
[4] *Il giornalino di Gian Burrasco* [The Diary of Johnny Hurricane] by Vamba (the pseudonym of Luigi Bertelli, 1858–1920), is a children's book about the comic misadventures of a badly behaved small boy.

Il giornalino di Gian Burrasco. It would be worthwhile to do a bit of research into it. I can only remember the word *Bube*, which means boy. My sister and I would say, 'Papa, read us Bube'. And he would read to us, translating as he went along.

Did he tell you that it was plagiarized?

When *Il giornalino di Gian Burrasco* was published, he told us, 'But this has been copied'.

A very attractive person, your father.

He was attractive to a lot of people, he was attractive to everyone I have spoken to. His relationship with me was not a close one. He wasn't what you would call a very attentive or affectionate father. He was proud of my scholastic achievements, but as a paternal relationship in the true sense of the word, a protective, encouraging, involved relationship, it was rather lacklustre.

So you don't have many memories of him as a father.

When he passed away I was twenty one. No, he passed away in '42, I was twenty-three. I didn't feel much grief for him.

Did you ever go for walks together?

No, he hated going for walks, he was an urban man, a city dweller. If he took us for a walk it was in Via Po, it would never have entered his head to take us for a walk in the country. He didn't like the countryside, he had no interest in nature. When he went to the country, the usual country retreats of Bardonecchia, Meana and Torre

Pellice,[5] he would just read or else play cards. He used to make us play tarot;[6] he had taught us to play tarot and expected us to play tarot with him, which we did, though without much interest.

At least you humoured him …

He taught us the games of his childhood. He bought a spinning top and showed us how it works, how to make it spin, which isn't easy, how to attack other people's tops with the whip of your own top. He taught us how to make a *s-ciopèt*[7] from a branch of elder.

How does a 's-ciopèt' work?

It's a hollowed-out branch of elder which you plug with two wads, one of which is a projectile and the other is a compressor, you push the second one in to make the first one shoot out.

Not an entirely predictable man.

He was rather a childish man. I don't think he was a good husband to my mother. He was worldly, he enjoyed

---

[5] Bardonecchia, Meana and Torre Pellice are all towns about fifty kilometres to the west of Turin, near the French border. Turinese children such as Primo Levi and his sister would typically have spent their summer holidays in or near the mountains (just as British children would spend theirs by the sea), and Levi would later return to Bardonecchia to indulge his passion for mountain sports.

[6] Tarot card games originated in Italy in the fifteenth century before spreading to France and other European countries. Piedmont has its own version of these games, called *tarocco*, which are played with a pack of seventy-eight cards.

[7] S-ciopèt is a dialect form of *schioppétta*, a disparaging term for a small, ineffective firearm. Cesare Levi's *s-ciopèt* was a popgun.

company, going to the theatre. My mother was very reserved, she was fifteen years younger than him.

But was theirs (forgive me if this is an indiscreet question) an arranged marriage?

Yes, it was arranged by relatives they had in common. My father was what they call a brilliant man, who promised to have a good career, as indeed he did. My mother had been brought up in an extremely traditional way. I can't tell you if she was actually fascinated by this ever so brilliant engineer. Probably yes, because she was a young girl and he was an experienced man.

In any case your mother never talked to you about it.

No.

Returning for a moment to religious education, did your mother act in a different way? Was she more inclined to respect Jewish traditions?

Traditions, yes, but not religious ones in particular.

So she didn't belong to a religious family either?

It's strange. My maternal grandfather was a traditional person, including religiously, he used to go to temple and celebrate the feasts. My mother strangely didn't inherit this, but of course you know that women count for little in the Jewish tradition, not much is delegated to women.

If it makes sense to ask the question, which of them influenced you more?

Undoubtedly my mother more than my father.

Was she there for you more?

I would say that my father influenced me genetically because he passed on to me a certain thirst for knowledge, by his own example as well. He supplied me with a lot of books, I only had to mention that I wanted a book and it would appear. From my mother I must have inherited a certain prudence, but it is hard to talk about these things. My mother is still alive ...

It's not essential for us to talk about it.

And besides these are things which are easier to see from the outside rather than the inside. Certainly my mother and I share a reputation for wisdom, I don't know how well deserved, because we don't run before we can walk. My father tended to run before he could walk. On the other hand, I can't explain why I, for example, took up mountaineering, without ever becoming really expert, but in a completely crazy and reckless way. I don't know who I got that from, indeed I recollect that my father and mother completely disapproved. It was a way of getting my own back, a rebellion.

Or even just a touch of foolhardiness inherited from your ancestors?

Ah, yes, it's possible that it came down to me from my distant forebears. However, the ones I knew personally were not like that, though I've heard stories about the others. Mark you – as you know – those ancestors I described[8] were ancestors in an extremely broad sense of

[8] Levi is referring to 'Argon', the opening chapter of *The Periodic Table (1975)*, 'a book about chemistry and chemists'. 'Argon' is,

the term, since I also allowed myself to borrow the ancestors of other people belonging to the community, to *ha
keillah*.

Shall we talk a bit about your paternal grandparents?

I never knew my paternal grandfather. He committed
suicide, though I don't know the circumstances, I don't
know if it was because of financial problems. I have his
name, I'm called Michele like him.

Michele?

Yes, Primo Michele, two names. I don't know anything
about him, though I've seen a portrait of him, I've seen
his graduation thesis, he was an engineer too.

A family tradition.

I don't think he worked as an engineer, I think he owned
some land in Benevagienna[9] which he managed. I don't
know anything about his suicide, nor have I ever wanted
to. As for my paternal grandmother, I described her in *The
Periodic Table*, and there isn't much to add, she was not an
agreeable woman. There were some photographs from the

precisely, an account of his ancestors, real and fictitious (that is to
say, not derived from family memories in the strict sense, but from
stories gathered from a wider narrative field). A rather absurd
and fantastic account of which Alberto Caviglion has offered an
illuminating reading – based on a typed copy given to him by Levi
– in his essay 'Argon e la cultura ebraica piemontese' [Argon and
Piedmontese Jewish culture] in *Primo Levi. Il presente del passato*
[Primo Levi: The Presence of the Past] (1991). (GT)
[9] Benevagienna, originally the Roman city of Augusta Bagiennorum,
is in the Piedmontese Province of Cuneo, about sixty kilometres
south of Turin.

end of the nineteenth century, some of which I still have somewhere. She was very beautiful. Then she got married again to a Christian doctor. Mixed marriages were more common than they are now. I was very frightened of her.

Mixed marriages were more common than they are now?

Yes, emancipation created an opening for it, many relatives that I have heard about made mixed marriages.

And you think that is no longer the case?

I can't say, I don't have the figures. After the war and after the racial laws[10] it was decisively the case. The racial laws turned the Jewish community back in on itself. It never entered anyone's mind to marry outside the Jewish circle. Or it entered the minds of very few.

What did the other two brothers do?

One was an ophthalmologist, and he too was a *bon viveur*. All three of them were. He was married to a very restless woman, very uneasy ...

What were they called?

My father was called Cesare, the ophthalmologist was Mario, and then there was Enrico, who was a broker. He lived in Genoa, and he was a very restless man as well. He was the least educated of the three brothers because he didn't have a degree, but all the same he had a fabulous library, including rare books, and he read a great deal.

---

[10] Laws passed by the Fascist regime between 1938 and 1943 which stripped Italian Jews of their civil rights.

A constant.

A constant in my father's family.

And on your mother's side?

My maternal grandfather was a patriarch, he was called Cesare too, Cesare Sarti. He was an obese giant of a man, a very good businessman. He had worked as a salesman in a fabric shop, in Via Roma, which he then took over and ran successfully for many years. He was a wealthy man, he bought a villa in Piossasco[11] which we used to visit for many years. He had six children, and my mother was his eldest daughter.

Excuse me for interrupting, but with regard to his brothers, your father was ...

He was the eldest too, the firstborn. The story goes that I was called Primo[12] because I was the firstborn offspring of two firstborn children.

Your grandfather Sarti's six children? Could you list them for me?

Yes, of course. My mother was the eldest. She was a housewife, the queen of the house in the traditional manner, which could sometimes be quite painful for my wife, living here with my mother, and so my wife became the queen of the house when my mother had to abdicate. The second sister is called Ida, she's still alive, she's ninety years old.

---

[11] Piossasco is a Piedmontese town about twenty kilometres south-west of Turin.
[12] Primo means 'first' in Italian.

The third was a schoolmistress. She emigrated to Brazil during the war. She was called Nella, and was an extremely lively, good-humoured, likeable, cheerful woman. She died of cancer.

At what age?

In her mid-fifties. The fourth was a son, called Corrado, who died a few years ago and it would be worth saying a bit about him.

Was he elderly too when he died?

He died when he was quite elderly. He was a remarkable man, he never had an education because he refused to study. In spite of this he learnt to play as many instruments as he could, and had a smattering of several languages. He had done his military service in Rome and was well known because whenever he was off duty he used to go and play the piano in cinemas. He played whatever came into his head, he improvised. After the First World War, which he missed by the skin of his teeth since he had been born in 1900 and was seventeen years old, he became a salesman with his father in the fabric shop. However, he was one of the pioneers of cinema here in Turin; he was a friend of Pastrone,[13] he worked with Pastrone, making special effects and acting too on occasion. They all did a bit of everything. He had a Pathé Baby, that is to say a movie camera, and he made a film, inviting friends and relatives

---

[13] Giovanni Pastrone (1883–1959) was an influential Italian director, screenwriter, actor and technical innovator during the era of silent film. He is probably best known today for the 1914 film *Cabiria*, for which the writer Gabriele D'Annunzio wrote the subtitles and, for many years, took the credit.

to take part. He told me that it was he who had made the volcano in *The Last Days of Pompeii*[14] ... it was only so big, a model. He was also one of the pioneers of radio. Out of sheer mental disorganization and lack of discipline, he never teamed up with the big names of radio, but he built crystal sets and used them, he showed them to me, he had a workshop. He was also an adventurous man who – since people didn't travel in those days – went in for dangerous rock climbing, he swam very well, he was one of the first people to own a motorbike, and my grandfather promised him a car if my mother's first child was a boy. And since I was a boy, he got a car thanks to me.

And was he grateful to you for that?

Yes, he was grateful to me, he often took me for drives, and in any case he later changed his car many times.

The fifth?

The fifth brother was the shadow of the fourth. There is not much to say about him. He was called Gustavo. It was intended that he should be a student, but he didn't study very much. He was the only one to go to the *ginnasio*,[15] but he did the first year and then dropped out. He was a shadow, a very unassuming man who tried to imitate his brother without much success. They sent him on ocean cruises several times in the hope that he would find a wife. He too died a few years ago. The sixth sister is still alive. She has always been very lively and vivacious, and perhaps

---

[14] This was a popular subject in Italian silent cinema. Corrado's volcano probably appeared in the 1926 film of that name, directed by Carmine Gallone and Amleto Palermi.
[15] See note 3 on p. 6.

the most intelligent of the six. She was left a widow tragically young, she just had time to bring two children into the world and then she was widowed and brought up those two children heroically, working as hard as she possibly could. During the war she had to hide them and herself. Those children were eight or nine years old, it was very hard to teach them that their name was not Segre.[16] Nevertheless, she survived, along with her two children. She's been quite distant now for the last four years.

Do you still see her?

Yes, I still see her.

And is she still lucid and lively?

Yes, she is very lucid.

So her memory is still sharp.

Yes, she has the family memory.

Would it be possible to approach her ....

She has already been approached, because she took part with great enthusiasm in a television broadcast which later was cut, in that programme of Caracciolo's.[17] She was

---

[16] An Italian Jewish surname which would have given away their ethnic identity.
[17] In his television documentary, *Il coraggio e la pietà. Gli ebrei e gli italiani durante la guerra* [Courage and Pity. The Jews and the Italians during the War] (RAI 1986), the journalist Nicola Caracciolo interviewed Jewish survivors of the Nazi-Fascist persecution, including Primo Levi.

recorded for that programme, but later her part, which was really good, was cut.

I asked you that on my own account, because I would like to hear other accounts of your family.

It wouldn't be a good time, because she has very bad arthritis in her leg.

I don't mean right away, but perhaps sometime later ...

Unfortunately by now those memories belong to people who can no longer hold on to them. Well, my mother still remembers things, but she doesn't want to, she's tired. One source, one of the principal sources of my information about the family, was the husband of the second sister, Ida. He too had boarded with a rabbi, and he remembered a great many things. He told me a lot of anecdotes which I later wrote down, and he led a curious life because he belonged to the only Jewish family in Venasca, near to Saluzzo, on the way to the Val Varaita. He lived the same life as the lads of his own age, in spite of being Jewish, which is to say going on endless bicycle rides, going to the mountains, going with women, apart from observing the feasts, celebrating the feasts, because in his family that was required. He was a handsome man and he described himself as a bit of a Don Juan. He had been in the First World War, he had caught malaria ...

In short, in your family there was this cultural and intellectual curiosity.

Yes.

And also a technical and scientific bent, it seems to me.
For example, you have recorded that your father preferred
Verne to Salgari.[18]

Yes, indeed. Verne was more serious.

Shall we move on now to talk about your childhood?
What memories do you have of your childhood?

I have some very early memories, I have one that is almost
certainly from when I was a year old, a memory, which I
might be able to check, from when I was a year old and I
was in Torre Pellice and they destroyed an ant-hill in front
of me, I don't know how I could check that, but I'm sure
that's where it was, in Torre Pellice, and that I must have
been a year old. I have a few inconsequential memories.
For instance, one time when I had a graze on my hand,
and a peasant woman said, '*Che dròlo!*'[19] and I asked my
Mamma what '*che dròlo*' meant. I had some playmates
that I later lost touch with. I have memories going back to
my early childhood which, while I'm not sure how happy
it was, was a tranquil one, tranquil until I was fourteen
or fifteen years old.

You were talking about country holidays in Torre Pellice,
Bardonecchia and Meana. Did you go to a different place
every year? Did you rent somewhere or did you own a house?

Yes, we used to rent a house, we took lodgings. We used
to stay in the country for three months.

---

[18] Unsurprisingly, Levi's father prefers the science fiction of Jules
Verne (1828–1905) to the swashbuckling pirate adventures in the
popular pulp fiction of Emilio Salgari (1862–1911).
[19] 'How odd!' The Piedmontese dialect word '*dròlo*' is derived from
the French word *drôle*, but means strange rather than comic.

So your life as a child was divided in two: time in the country and time spent in the city and at school.

Almost all my memories are of the country, because school was boring. Yes, almost all my memories are of the country, I remember Torre Pellice quite well, I remember Bardonecchia, I remember Meana.

Have you been back to those country holiday places of yours?

Yes, and I found them smaller than I remembered, as often happens. Nowadays those places have completely changed.

But there must be a few things which have stayed the same.

Yes, a few things have stayed the same, the landscapes have stayed the same.

But is there anything which makes you say, 'Goodness, this is exactly how I remember it'?

The mountains of Bardonecchia.

Any paths or spots which are special places?

I've been back there so seldom.

You don't suffer from nostalgia?

No.

And how were those country holiday places chosen?

Holiday places were chosen on account of the railway. My father couldn't stand the heat in Turin so he looked for places he could get back to every evening. And since the trains only went to Torre Pellice, Bardonecchia and the Val di Susa, the choice fell on those.

I asked you that because I was thinking of Croce's stays in Meana.[20]

It was the same for everyone, the convenience of the railway. There was a station there, and not in Susa.

Were there no cars?

No indeed, not even wealthy families went there by car, because there was no infrastructure then, no garages or petrol stations. You had to be very daring to have a car, and you also had to have a chauffeur.

Did you play with other children? Did you have anyone to play with in your family?

My sister was my chief companion.

What is the age difference between you?

A year and a half.

What is she called?

Anna Maria.

---

[20] From 1924 to1937, the Italian philosopher, historian, art critic and liberal politician Benedetto Croce spent the summers with his wife in the beautiful and peaceful surroundings of Meana in the Susa Valley, partly to escape as far as possible from the surveillance of the Fascist regime.

A year and a half is fine when it comes to playing together, isn't it?

Very fine indeed, and we shared such a close childhood together that it brings back a flood of memories. We remind each other by turns about the things we said and did, and the people we met, an intimacy which has never ceased.

It's this wealth of memories that I feel I've been observing.

A wealth of memories, yes, but I've squandered it all now, I've worked my way through almost all of them and I have hardly anything left.

That's not how it seems to me.

To me it seems to me as if I've said all that I can possibly say, but I ought to add a few things, a few episodes. I was a pest of a boy who always had influenza or a sore throat or a stomach ache, one thing or another, so my parents decided to let me take the first year of *ginnasio* privately. I was taught arts subjects by Zino Zini's daughter, Marisa Zini,[21] and mathematics by my old schoolmistress, a delightful person ...

---

[21] Zino Zini (1868–1937) was a moral philosopher of a positivist bent, and a believer in socialism (as a socialist he was a municipal councillor in Turin between 1906 and 1919). He concerned himself with Darwinism, Marxism and criminal anthropology (but also with poetry: in 1926 he published *Poetry and Truth*), and he was a lecturer in moral philosophy at the University of Turin. He was a correspondent for *Il Gazzetta del Popolo*, *La Stampa*, *L'Avanti!*, and the Gramscian *Ordine Nuovo*. He taught history and philosophy at the Liceo D'Azeglio up to the school year 1934–35. Maria Luisa (Marisa) Zini, of whom we are speaking, herself taught arts subjects in the D'Azeglio lower school from 31 October 1930. (GT)

About whom we must talk, along with the rest of your experiences at elementary school.

Elementary school! I was permanently second in the class.

Did you start in the usual way, at six years old.

Yes, at six years old.

I don't know why, but I was convinced that you had started a year early.

No, for health reasons, because I wouldn't say I was a sickly child, but I always had something the matter with me, and I was delicate. My sister, who was younger than me, was taller than I was.

So she had fewer problems.

Yes, fewer problems. I remember being very bored by the school curriculum because they taught me things I already knew.

Where did you go?

To the Rignon Elementary School, in Via Massena.

For all five years?

Four years, because I skipped the fifth year.

With the same schoolmistress?

No, I also had a stupid and boring schoolmaster.

Do you remember his name?

No, I don't remember it.

Young or old?

He seemed very old to me. He must have been forty years old.

Why did you find him stupid and boring?

For a specific reason. I remember very clearly a question I asked him. I asked him whether a strong man would be able to throw a stone horizontally and he replied that yes he could, and he drew a straight line on the blackboard, saying at the end, 'But then it falls'. Because that's wrong, it can't be done. Not even the strongest man in the world can throw a stone horizontally. I knew that was the case, so I was testing him out.

You were leading him on.

Yes, I was leading him on. But I don't remember anything else. I remember that his lessons were boring.

Did you have marked likes and dislikes?

I had a strong liking for my schoolmistress, for my schoolmistress Emilia Glauda, who died only a few years ago, at a great age, and who was an angelic person. She still used to wear long skirts, almost down to her ankles.

So she knew about your achievements as a writer.

Yes, yes, she wrote to me in her marvellous handwriting.

Would you like to tell me a bit about her?

I can't say much more except that she was an extremely affectionate, patient person, a teacher out of the novel *Cuore*,[22] a little schoolmistress who was dedicated to her job. She was unmarried.

Was she young then?

She must have been thirty-five.

Your grades in elementary school?

As I told you, I was second in the class, I always had good marks.

Who was top of the class? Do you remember?

Yes, he was called Aldo Conti. I met him again a few years ago, a fine boy, very bright, very intelligent.

Second for all four years?

Yes, for all four years.

The eternal second?

Yes, but it's not as if I was trying to come first.

---

[22] *Cuore* [Heart], a popular children's book with a nine-year-old schoolboy protagonist, was published in 1886 by Edmondo De Amicis (1846–1908). Set in Turin after the unification of Italy, it combines left-wing social and moral concerns with an attempt to inculcate patriotism and civic virtues in its young readers.

What was your reaction? What do you remember about it?

Nothing but boredom.

You kept your school reports, I expect.

No, I never kept them. I think we had to hand them
back. There were no grades on the reports, but there were
comments: 'excellent', 'satisfactory'. I oscillated between
excellent and good.

The subjects which you liked best?

I don't really remember ...

History?

No, I hated history. I always hated it, unfortunately, and I'm
still ignorant about history. Geography interested me a little.
I remember an incident which happened in the first or second
year to do with a *pensierino* ...[23] perhaps in the second year,
yes. They had told me to write six *pensierini* about the sun. I
wrote all six condensed into a single sentence, I wrote, 'The
sun gives light and heat, the sun is the brightest star in the
sky' and I don't really remember what else. The schoolmistress pointed out to me that *pensierino* means a sentence, so
I had only written one. I was condemned to write another
five *pensierini* and it was very difficult.

---

[23] The word *pensierino*, literally a small thought, also means a sentence. Writing *pensierini* – a series of short sentences on an assigned
theme – was an early exercise in composition for elementary school
pupils.

Economy of words ...

I also remember the difficulty I had in writing commas, because I tried to write commas like the ones in printed books, that is to say a dot with a tail, and I wrote enormous commas because I was struggling to reproduce their typographic form in printed books. I had already started to read before that and when I went to school I already knew how to read.

Perhaps your boredom was also because of that.

Yes, I already knew how to read because my mother and father had taught me. I had a passion, not in the least reciprocated, for teaching everything to my sister, who couldn't care less, it meant nothing to her. She was much more sporty than me, she was much livelier than me, and it bored her to listen. She wouldn't listen to me at all, she just made fun of me.

What did your sister do later on?

She also went to the *ginnasio* and then the *liceo*, but her time at *liceo* was cut short by the racial laws. She finished her schooling at the Jewish *liceo* and she graduated after the war in Literature and History of Art.

And then did she teach?

No, she has never taught, She got a job with Olivetti and followed a career there.[24]

---

[24] Anna Maria Levi edited *The International Review of Community Development*, a journal created by the industrialist, idealist and politician Adriano Olivetti (1901–1960).

I should like to return for a moment to the subject of your domestic servant, which we dropped to talk of other things. You told me that she was delightful.

She was a very devout woman. For a year or two we slept in the same room.

Do you remember her name?

Silvia Meneghelli.

Was she from Turin?

No, she came from Fiorenzuola d'Arda.[25] She was devoted to Saint Rita, indeed she took part in the novenas to Saint Rita, she contributed her modest offerings to the church, and in the evenings she would pray, she would kneel down and pray.

Did she stay with you for many years?

As far as I can remember, at least from '24 to '34, ten years.

Did you have other domestic servants after her?

After my father fell ill, he had cancer and had to have surgery, we had to employ someone who could also nurse him, and Silvia Meneghelli was dismissed. We also had a maid-of-all-work who stayed with us as long as she could.

[25] A city and district in the province of Piacenza in Emilia-Romagna.

And in any case she didn't replace the other one.

She was a very exuberant woman from the Veneto.

Was Silvia Meneghelli old or young?

To me she seemed very old, she must have been fifty-five or sixty.

Was the next one younger?

Yes, she was younger.

Can we pick up the thread of your elementary school for a little longer? I imagine that your class was very large.

There were about thirty-five of us.

You talked about your dislike of history. What about arithmetic?

I liked it well enough. I used to play games on my own. I noticed that if you take any number, however long, and subtract it from the same number in reverse, you end up with a multiple of nine, but I never tried to work out why.

You discovered it intuitively?

I discovered it through playing.

You played with numbers.

Yes.

What about the natural sciences?

They had been cut, they were not taught. I was interested in them, but they were not taught.

Did you see yourself as rather precocious or did you feel that you were just like all the other children?

No, I was the most puny child and the smallest, as well as always coming second I was also the shortest in height. So I was always the first in line when we did gymnastics, something which I found humiliating.

However, you said there was no discrimination on account of your being Jewish.

I didn't feel that there was, I don't remember any such incident.

But you did feel there was a difference on account of your physique.

Yes, and I suffered from that for a very long time.

Was that just your own impression, or do you remember anyone trying to upset you about it?

At the *ginnasio*, yes, but not at elementary school, because there were also poor children there. There was a boy with rickets, there were poor people in short. In *ginnasio*, yes, it upset me a lot being so puny.

You said earlier that you played with numbers. Also with words?

Also with words.

On the subject of books: do you remember particular passages, comics, comic strips?

There weren't any comics in those days, there was the 'Corriere dei Piccoli',[26] which was almost required reading. Every family used to get it, and I would read it from the first page to the last and really enjoy it. As for the elementary school, I know that I had to put in quite a lot of effort to skip the fifth year, and it was my good fortune that I did because, if I hadn't skipped the fifth year, my education would later have been cut short by the racial laws.[27]

But did you skip the fifth year out of boredom or for some other reason?

No, it was my father and mother who decided that I should skip the fifth year.

And so you took the exam at the Rignon school as an external student and then went on to the ginnasio?

Yes, to the D'Azeglio.[28] But as I told you, I did my first year of *ginnasio* privately.

---

[26] The *Corriere dei Piccoli* [Children's Courier] was a weekly magazine for children, included as a supplement in the newspaper *Corriere della Sera* and also for sale separately.

[27] Since Levi had already begun his university course when the racial laws were passed, the exclusion of Jewish students from state education did not apply to him and he was able to complete his first degree in chemistry, although he was prevented from taking a further degree or accepting an academic post.

[28] Levi spent his *ginnasio* and *liceo* years at the Liceo Classico Massimo D'Azeglio, one of the most prestigious secondary schools in Turin.

Yes of course, with Marisa Zini tutoring you. But with the ginnasio we are moving on to a new stage. Let's stay a little longer with your childhood, and with the books of your childhood. Cuore *for instance, did you read that?*

I was given *Cuore* as a prize, I can't remember in which class, it was the prize for the best students. It made very little impression on me, I didn't find it moving, I wasn't really convinced by it, I didn't take it to heart.

Were you a child who was easily moved or not?

I was a very sensitive child. I remember an incident which reduced me to floods of tears, when we read in the papers about Nobile's crash at the Pole.[29] The incident of a submarine which sank with men still alive inside it, who banged on the wall and it was impossible to rescue them, that made a tremendous impression on me and had me in tears. I was very frightened of skeletons, books with skulls in them caused me real physical discomfort.

Other books which you remember from your childhood?

I remember the titles. I remember *Flik o tre mesi in un circo*.[30] I read that before I went to school. I read *Pinocchio*, which I enjoyed.

[29] The Italian aviator and arctic explorer Umberto Nobile (1885–1978) made two flights over the North Pole, the second of which, in 1928, ended in a disastrous crash onto the ice north-northeast of Spitsbergen, killing seven members of the crew and also causing the death of Roald Amundsen, whose plane disappeared during the subsequent rescue mission.

[30] *Flik o tre mesi in un circo* [Flik or Three Months in a Circus] is a children's book by Emma Perodi (1850–1918) about the adventures of a small boy who runs away from home and joins a circus.

Did you read a lot or a little?

I was always reading, I always had a book supplied by my father.

Jumping backwards a little, you said that you were born here in this house.

I have a curious recollection, which is probably connected to the birth of my sister, so I must have been a year and a half old. A recollection of some kind of commotion, and of someone who picked me up in their arms and lifted me up and down in front of the curtains, and I saw the curtains moving. My mother was never ill, so if my mother was in bed she was probably in bed for the birth.

Since you were such a large family, were there often get-togethers when relatives came to your house?

Yes, it was a big family. Those brothers and sisters of my mother often used to come, they would come to visit us and we would go to their house. It was customary on a Sunday for all of the grandchildren to visit my maternal grandparents' house, there was a whole succession of us grandchildren, there were eleven of us in the end. Our uncle, the one who was involved in cinema, had set up a local movie theatre, and he used to put on shows for us in the corridor of films that he had hired I don't know where, after which he would take us home in his car, or sometimes in a coach. However, it was only a kilometre's distance so it wasn't much of a journey.

But all this didn't happen in Via Po?

No, it was my paternal grandparents who had a house in Via Po. My maternal grandparents lived in Corso Vittorio on the corner with Corso Re Umberto. We would be taken home in the car and there was always a competition because we always wanted to be the last to be taken home. That way the journey would last longer.

Was your house bought by your father?

It wasn't his, it was my mother's dowry, it was my mother's wedding present, her dowry.

Was it all fields here then?

Yes, nearly all fields. There was the Villa Rignon near here. I vaguely remember that we would go to watch the trains a little way beyond the Mauriziano Hospital, there was a level crossing.

What kind of memory do you think you have? Visual? Aural?

A memory of no specific kind. A memory that is partly visual and partly of spoken words, of things that I heard said. The nanny, the nursemaid, who said, 'Don't touch the buttercups or they'll make your nails fall out'. And that potatoes give you backache. Do you know why? It's a play on words: they give you backache because you have to bend over to harvest them.

Shall we see if we can come up with any other memories?

There is the *ginnasio* if you are interested in that.

Yes, of course.

I was ten or eleven years old, I collected stamps, I had some classmates ...

You had already entered the ginnasio *after the year in which you studied privately.*

Yes. I had a teacher in the first year, that is to say in the second and third years, because of course I didn't take the first year, a teacher who was intelligent but malicious.

We're in the ginnasio *of the old days, that is to say at the age corresponding to today's middle school.*[31]

In those days there was the lower *ginnasio* and the upper *ginnasio*, three years followed by two.

So we're talking about the lower ginnasio.

Yes. I had an intelligent teacher, I wouldn't say she was malicious but mischievous. She was quite a young woman and she kept her eye on me. I remember that since I did well at the *ginnasio*, and was now top of the class by quite a long way, she said to me, 'One day they'll put up a plaque in this classroom: Primo Levi studied here', something which made a strange impression on me.

And what was this teacher called?

Maria Borgogno.

But I know who that is, she's called Anna Borgogno.

Perhaps it was Anna ...

---

[31] Italian students now attend middle school for three years from the age of eleven, before going on to five years of *liceo*.

She lives in Rome, she wrote a novel, La città perduta,
which I actually reviewed, she was the niece of the writer
Vittorio Actis (Amilcare Solferini), she describes her child-
hood, the Fascist period, the difficulties that she had as a
democratic and nonconformist teacher.[32]

Yes, she was not a Fascist. She kept her eye on me, at all
events. She deliberately put me next to the stupidest boy,
I don't know why.

Certainly, by what one can deduce from her novel, she
wasn't a woman given to sentimentality.

She wrote me a letter, after *If This is a Man*, asking if I
was the Primo Levi who had been a pupil of hers and who
wrote compositions in very tiny handwriting which was
difficult to decipher, and I replied that yes, that was me,
but I think I must have lost that letter.

In any case, she moved to Rome.

Yes, and in Rome she was a librarian, but I don't know
where. Perhaps it is Anna Borgogno ...

Yes, it is Anna Borgogno.

She made me share a desk with the stupidest boy in the
class to see what would happen. She enjoyed making

---

[32] Anna Borgogno, who was thirty-two at the time, taught arts
subjects in years two and three of the *ginnasio*. Her personality,
although fictionalized, is contained in her novel *La città perduta*
[The Lost City], published in 1981 by Pan, in which – having
subsequently moved to Rome as a librarian – she describes the
stages of a life lived with pride and rigour, with a profound sense
of independence and of intellectual nonconformity. (GT)

experiments like that. Then, since it was a mixed class of boys and girls, she put me near to the girls to see what would happen. She made these experiments ...

And what did happen?

Nothing. I was very shy and withdrawn, I went red. There was one incident I remember well. We were talking about avarice, about somebody miserly ... Someone at the back of the class said, 'A Jew, in other words', and she was violently angry and told him, 'We don't say things like that'.

What did she teach?

She taught Italian, Latin, history and geography.

Your other teachers?

I had a very boring mathematics master who didn't know how to teach, and wasn't all that good at the subject himself. I was good at Latin, I really liked Latin. I was a 'grammaticus', I was interested in Latin grammar, I was already interested back then in the etymology of Italian words. I asked for an etymological dictionary as a present. However, I wrote good compositions when it was a question of making things up, that is to say creative writing, and I wrote really bad compositions when it was a question of critical writing, that is to say commenting on poems. I had absolutely no interest in poetry. Poems by Carducci and Pascoli became stuck in my memory, as they do. They are still stuck in my memory, but I didn't enjoy them.

While on the other hand with creative composition ...

I was good at it, I wrote entertaining compositions.

You haven't kept anything from that period?

Nothing.

Any photographs?

One or two photographs. I should say that ... well, yes,
I've just remembered a book that made a great impression on me, I read Jerome's *Three Men on the Bummel*,
and also *Three Men in a Boat*, and tried unconsciously to
imitate it in my writing.

You imitated the humour ...

Yes, I unconsciously tried to imitate it.

And did you succeed?

Ah, well, yes, I used to get ten out of ten for my compositions back then, in the lower *ginnasio*. In the upper *ginnasio*, on the other hand, when it was a question of essays
on Manzoni and Ariosto, that wasn't my kind of thing.

*Going back to your teachers, can you remember the name
of your mathematics teacher?*

Yes, Pandolfi.

His first name?

No.

Any other observations about Anna Borgogno?

Classmates who were more mature than me used to make
snide remarks about her. She used to hint at things, she

wasn't as candid as she wanted to appear. She was certainly an intelligent woman.

Literature, mathematics, not Greek yet though. Physical education?

Physical education in those days was the monopoly of Fascism.

But it was on the school syllabus?

Yes, the physical education teacher was a Fascist *gerarca*,[33] but he was a poor devil of a man, already elderly, who didn't know how to do gymnastics himself. He made us march and run and jump. I was rather weak but I was quite agile.

Other subjects? Drawing?

No, we didn't learn drawing. There was geometry, geometric drawing. I've never learnt to draw.

You haven't kept your reports from the ginnasio *either?*

No, none at all.

You weren't good at keeping hold of your possessions.

No, but above all, you know, there was the whole of the war after that, when who knows how many things were lost.

---

[33] The term *gerarca* [hierarch] was used of those who held prominent positions in the National Fascist Party.

Also because then you all had to go into hiding.

I was interned, my mother had to go into hiding, she had to scatter her things in the houses of Christian friends, who in some cases gave them back, and in some cases held onto them, the books were scattered in so many different places ...

So that's why you don't even have the books from your childhood any more.

Apart from just a few.

You do have some of them?

I still have some of them, I've kept about twenty of them. Look up there, the top shelf on the left, that row of bound books, that's where my father's books used to be and I don't know where those ended up.

With all the books he read, your father must have had a fine library.

A fine library, yes.

Which is now missing.

Nine tenths of it is missing.

Do you never feel sad about that loss?

Ah well, even the books that are left are all ruined, they've been rained on, they are just mementos, keepsakes.

Do you remember any of your ginnasio *classmates?*

One was Fernanda Pivano.[34]

Classmates you were close friends with?

Not with Fernanda Pivano, because she gave herself so many airs, she was older than me.

She put on airs?

It wasn't just that she put on airs. She was already well developed, as they say, and I wasn't. She was my classmate all through lower and upper *ginnasio*, for four years: five years minus one. No, I was never close to Fernanda Pivano. I've lost sight of the others along the way, occasionally I run into one of them.

No friend that you could confide in, that you could spend time with in the afternoons?

I had a friend like that, yes, but we'll come back to him because he had a terrible fate. Going back to the *ginnasio*, he was in the parallel class to mine, he was Jewish too. We became friends and did lots of things together. Now he has a mental illness, a very sad business.

---

[34] Fernanda Pivano (1919–2009) was a translator, critic and journalist who was influential in introducing contemporary American writers, including Ernest Hemingway, William Faulkner and John Dos Passos, and later the poets and musicians of the Beat Generation, to an Italian audience.

How did you spend your free time? Did you already go on trips to the mountains?

In those days, when I was at the *ginnasio*, trips to the mountains were a family affair, in fact everybody went on them, though not my father.

He used to arrive in the evening ...

Not my father, he didn't like walking, but my mother took us for walks, she liked the mountains. There would be little excursions, bathing in the Angrogna near Torre Pellice and walks through the fields. My mother has a certain talent for recognizing plants, she taught us the names of the plants, but especially my sister, I had an extremely close relationship with my sister. I used to play games with ants, that's to say I tried to find out what an ant would do if it was in difficulties, but without ever killing one. I would set up a barrier, I would put a leaf with a hole in it over an ant, the ant would have to get out through the hole and climb onto the leaf, and then I would float the leaf in a basin of water with a twig to see if the ant would manage to find the twig. I kept tadpoles, but I've already described that ...

You carried out little experiments, applying the experimental method.

No, but I read Darwin very early, I can't say when. I've kept that edition of Darwin, perhaps I read it when I was fifteen or sixteen years old.

So that's how you found out about natural selection.

Yes, it made a great impression on me. Especially the vigour of the argument.

Here, though, we have practically reached your first year of liceo.

Yes.

And have you seen Fernanda Pivano since then?

Yes, I saw her once, I once went to a talk she gave and made myself known to her. She also recently sent me her regards.

She has written a novel.

Yes, she has written a novel but I haven't read it.

Back to your teachers. In the ginnasio, *did you always have the same teachers?*

I had Anna Borgogno for two years in the lower *ginnasio*, then in the upper *ginnasio* I had a very disagreeable teacher, he was called Taverna, I don't remember his first name. He was very strict, taught badly and had no love for young people. He was very harsh, I have unpleasant memories of him. I remember that together with my schoolmates we would think up the most terrible tortures to punish his callousness. He taught Italian, Latin, Greek, history and geography.

Was moving from the lower ginnasio *to the upper* ginnasio *painful for you?*

Well yes, because of Anna Borgogno, and also because she was a woman and the other was a man, it was a bit like leaving your mother's lap, and then it was the beginning of a difficult period for me, because my schoolmates had begun to be interested in girls and in sex and I was not. I was very backward in that respect, I felt terribly inhibited, terribly backward and I had made a curious vow to myself, telling myself in a Darwinian way: there are two possibilities, either I am capable of reproduction or I am not. If I am not, then nothing doing, I don't even want to try; if I am, then it will develop by itself, it will begin by itself, it will happen by itself.

That seems to me a mature way of thinking.

I should say that, from then on, that unhappy period in my life began which went on right up to and including Auschwitz and was only resolved afterwards. That is to say that I led the life of an inhibited person which I suffered from terribly and which was just what I tried to compensate for with mountaineering, practised in a reckless way, with violent sports, with running and cycling, all those things. But my schoolmates jeered at me because they realized I was different.

You didn't have the same desires and urges as them.

They didn't talk about anything else, they told dirty jokes and my sexual education took place through dirty jokes and Freud.

Meaning?

My father had given me books by Mantegazza[35] and Freud; he made absolutely no attempt to lend me a hand, to come to my aid.

---

[35] Paolo Mantegazza (1831 1910) was an Italian neurologist, anthropologist and social Darwinist whose racial theories make his work an ironic addition to Levi's early reading. Best known for his defence of the use of cocaine, he also wrote about sexual

Basically, he left you to fend for yourself.

Worse than that, he used to taunt me. He, who had led a completely different life, used to say to me, 'What are you waiting for to get yourself a girl?'

Not showing much sensitivity.

My sister had started having flirtations …

relations. Cesare Levi gave his son *The Physiology of Love* (1896), in which Mantegazza 'studied the body as a kind of laboratory in which physiological processes took place' out of which 'love arises metaphorically as a mysterious creative chemistry between two unequal atoms', with women, 'dominated by what Mantegazza calls "the ideology of sacrifice"' as definitely the less equal and less intelligent partners. (Dolores Martín Moruno, 'Love in the time of Darwinism: Paolo Mantegazza and the emergence of sexuality', *Medicina & Storia*, X, 2010, 19–20, n.s., pp. 147–164, p. 156.) Unsurprisingly, Mantegazza's book offered little help to a shy and troubled adolescent boy.

Monday, 26 January

Last time we got as far as talking about the ginnasio. *Shall we talk now about your time in* liceo?

At that time being a student at the D'Azeglio was a privilege, because the D'Azeglio was renowned for being a good *liceo*, and not only that but it was secretly renowned for being an anti-fascist *liceo*. As a matter of fact, by my time, there had been a clean sweep of the anti-fascist teachers, at least those openly so, and there wasn't a single one left.

During which years?

The years '34, '35 and '36.

You have talked about your generation as a generation which no longer had teachers.

Without teachers that we had direct contact with, or, to put it a better way, there were some teachers. There was

Umberto Cosmo,[36] for instance, who had been a teacher
at the D'Azeglio but had been reduced to silence. He was
a grand old man, dignified but shy, and it was obvious
that they wanted to make his life difficult. There was the
memory of Zino Zini, there was the memory of Pavese, of
Antonicelli, the memory of Monti of course.[37] But word of
them never reached me, nobody talked about them, and
those who knew stayed silent.

[36] The literary critic Umberto Cosmo (1868–1944), taught Italian
and Latin in Turin at the Liceo Classico Gioberti and at the
D'Azeglio, where Piero Gobetti and Norberto Bobbio were students
of his. As a university lecturer in Italian literature, still in Turin,
Antonio Gramsci was a student of his with whom he developed
a friendship which was not without strong disagreements (later
magnanimously resolved in a memorable embrace which Gramsci
has described). Originally a socialist and later a progressive liberal,
he was always an anti-fascist, subjected to the persecution of the
regime which in 1926 prohibited him from teaching and in 1929
condemned him to internal exile. He was a distinguished Dante
scholar, among whose books at least his *Vita di Dante* [Life of
Dante] (1930) and *L'ultima ascesa. Introduzione alla lettura del
'Paradiso'* [The Final Ascent: An Introduction to Reading *Paradiso*]
(1936) have survived. (GT)
[37] For Zino Zini, see note 21 on p. 21. Franco Antonicelli (1902–
1974) was a fine essayist, writer and poet. As an anti-fascist, in
1935 he was condemned to internal exile, but in 1936, after being
liberated, he founded the Da Silva publishing firm, which in 1947
published the first edition of *If This is a Man*. Augusto Monti
(1881–1966) was almost *the* teacher *par excellence* of the D'Azeglio,
about which he wrote in the chapter 'Scuola di Resistenza, 1923–
32' [School of Resistance, 1923–32], included in his memoirs of
scholastic life, *I miei conti con la scuola* [My Tales of School Life]
(1965), republished in the volume *Il mestiere di insegnare* [The
Trade of Teaching] (1994). It may not be out of place to mention
that Giovanni Tesio has given an account of Augusto Monti, intellectual, teacher and writer, in his book, *Augusto Monti. Attualità
di un uomo all'antica* [Augusto Monti: The Life and Times of an
Old-Fashioned Man] (L'Arciere, Cuneo 1980). (GT)

Things that you learnt later?

There were whispers that I didn't understand. Also because I wasn't an anti-fascist and neither was I a Fascist. I was bourgeois, a young bourgeois boy, the son of a bourgeois family. My father was a politically prudent man, he had witnessed the Hungarian revolution and it had given him such a shock that he disliked communism, and revolutions in general, and revival movements in general. He didn't like Fascism either, he was essentially a liberal, but he kept quiet about it and had absolutely no influence on my political education.

So there was no discussion of politics at home.

No, my father used to curse when he had to put on his black shirt. He had chosen the path of least resistance and joined the party, so he had to go and vote 'yes' or 'no', which is to say 'yes', because he was a card-carrying member, you know how it went ... So he was repelled by Fascism, but you couldn't call him an anti fascist.

A malcontent.

Yes.

And so you, when you went to school ...

I did everything according to the school rules, I joined the *balilla* according to the rules, and then the *avanguardisti*,[38]

---

[38] The Opera Nazionale Balilla was a paramilitary youth movement in which the Fascist regime enrolled children between the ages of eight and fourteen, after which they became *avanguardisti* until the age of eighteen.

and I too was a malcontent because I thoroughly disliked all that marching about, it didn't involve anything positive. Fascist doctrine, however, I can't deny that it had a certain appeal. That idealized version of Fascism as a life force, as a vital impetus,[39] did have a certain appeal. Not enough to make me sign up, but enough to make me calmly able to swallow, for example, the war in Ethiopia. I had a map of Ethiopia with the flags. Like the majority of Italians, I believed in it.

It was the high point of the myth.

Yes, the high point of the Fascist myth which fell apart soon afterwards.

There was a remarkable popular consensus.

I was fifteen years old.

Yes, I understand that. I am talking of the consensus of the adults.

Something which was no longer the case with Spain. In the Spanish war that followed it was immediately clear that popular consensus was lacking. It was a bloodthirsty war, the Spanish one, deaths on both sides, and Italians on both sides, and that came to be public knowledge.

---

[39] The term *élan vital*, coined by the French philosopher Henri Bergson (1859–1941), was translated as *slancio vitale* [vital impetus] and used by advocates of Fascism such as Giovanni Gentile to suggest the dynamism and historical inevitability of the rise of the Fascist state under its destined, heroic leader, Mussolini.

But how did it make you feel, all this ideology about the vital impetus, when you describe yourself as someone who was shy and out of place?

I did feel shy, I did feel out of place, and I didn't feel like a Fascist. Above all, my teachers may not have been anti-fascist but neither were they Fascists, with the exception of one half crazy poor devil of a philosophy teacher who was a Fascist but was so stupid that he made a laughing stock both of himself and of the Fascism that he preached. Our Italian teacher was the well-known Azelia Arici,[40] who was not a Fascist, though she did have her weaknesses, and who adhered to an essentially decent programme of studies in Italian, based on the classics, in some small homage secretly offered to the memory of her predecessors. Secretly.

Do you remember your other teachers?

Yes, of course. Coccolo,[41] the Greek and Latin master, was an excellent Latinist and Greekist. He was a priest,

[40] Azelia Arici (1895–1978) was Primo Levi's Italian teacher during his three secondary school years (from 1934–35 to 1936–37). She won her professorship in Italian and Latin in 1925. She taught in Bergamo, in Casale Monferrato, in Carmagnola and finally at the D'Azeglio in Turin, in the post which had belonged to Augusto Monti. She was an expert on Catullus, Dante, Alfieri, Collodi and Dino Buzzati, and translated the complete works of Tacitus (published between 1952 and 1959). (GT)
[41] There is a fine description of Lorenzo Coccolo, the Latin and Greek master at the D'Azeglio from the school year 1927–28, in the chapter 'Testimonianza per due maestri' [An Account of Two Schoolmasters] in Luigi Firpo's book *Gente di Piemonte* [The People of Piedmont]: 'the arts subjects – Italian and Latin, history and philosophy – were still thought of in those days as masculine disciplines, and the only one of my teachers who wore a skirt did

there's a picture of him in your book, *Viaggio nella città*.[42] Unfortunately he was a rather ridiculous person because he drank a lot. His scholarship was remarkable but his way of expounding it was intrinsically ridiculous. He was already a ridiculous figure in any case, because he was very small, with a red face and childishly blue eyes, with a thick Piedmontese accent, and he actually spoke in Piedmontese sometimes when the words slipped out. I remember that once when someone was causing trouble he said, '*Chi ch'a l'é ch'a romp le bale?*' After which he publicly apologized, saying, 'I was compelled to use a rather improper word.'[43] That's what he was like, so he was an estimable person, but ridiculous at the same time.

And did Don Coccolo teach you Greek and Latin in your first, second and third year?

Yes, in the first, second and third year.

So there were no changes in those three years?

No.

so not on account of being female but in adherence to canon law, because we are speaking of a little, mild-natured, vigorous country priest, with a purple nose which he often used to blow into a big red and white checked handkerchief: this was Don Lorenzo Còccolo, who must have had a more than sufficient knowledge of Latin and Greek, but was completely incapable of teaching it to us, idle and self-indulgent profiteers from his defenceless innocence' (Milan: Mursia, 1983, pp. 289–92). (GT)

[42] Augusto Monti, *Viaggio nella Città. Antologia di pagine torinese* [A Journey round the City: An anthology of Turinese pages], ed. Giovanni Tesio (Turin: Famija Turèisa, 1977).

[43] The improper word was *bale* [balls]; a corresponding English idiom is 'Who's being such a pain in the arse?'

Did Azelia Arici teach you Italian for three years?

Yes.

And in mathematics?

Yes, that was Maria Mascalchi, a fine woman. She wasn't a great mathematician, but she had a certain talent as a teacher. She was fair, she never did anything openly unjust, she was in command of her material, a dependable person.

Philosophy and history?

For a year we had Professor Eusebietti. He was an authority on Aristotle and had translated Aristotle into Italian, but I remember him as distant, he didn't connect with us. Every now and then he would make us laugh, but any kind of personal connection was out of the question. Apart from anything else, you have to remember that we were an enormous class of forty-one students, all boys and mostly rascals, so we were unmanageable in short. Even the professor couldn't control a class like that. For the following two years we had a teacher called Gerbaz, from the Val d'Aosta, one of those teachers who make themselves a laughing stock. He was continually making mistakes, not just in pronunciation but also in the course material he prepared. I don't know how he could have ... in fact there was talk later of his being hospitalized. His teaching was quite worthless.

What other subjects are left?

Natural sciences, for which there was an elderly lady called Pangella, whom I constantly challenged because I knew more about chemistry than she did, I had already studied it on my own, and I used to ask her embarrassing questions which she didn't know how to reply to. I can remember some of my malicious questions which I knew the answer to already, but she would give the wrong answer.

On a different level, the same kind of behaviour that you talked about in relation to your elementary schoolmaster. From what you are saying, it doesn't seem to me that the D'Azeglio was such a good school. It doesn't seem that there were all that many memorable teachers.

Azelia Arici. She was a memorable teacher, so much so that I still remember some of her lessons now. She struggled with that class of delinquents, struggled desperately. All the same, objectively speaking, I have to admit that she was an excellent teacher. Yet she didn't manage to capture my imagination because my interest lay elsewhere, it was already fixed on chemistry.

Apart from the very early days, when did that vocation begin?

Pretty well in my first year of *liceo*. I set myself up with the chemical products which I could find at home, and I found some chemistry textbooks and my father also gave me some, I performed silly little experiments which I thought were amazing, ones from the time of the alchemists, the tree of Venus, the tree of Jupiter, the tree of Mars, I crystallized salts.[44]

[44] The branching crystalline structures which the alchemists called the vegetation of metals are formed by adding different metal salts to waterglass (an aqueous solution of sodium silicate), which was a common household chemical in Levi's youth, as it was used to preserve eggs.

But this all started outside school, without any scholastic stimulus.

Yes.

Was there a reason?

Out of curiosity. Because I was interested in the starry sky, I was interested in animals, I used to raise tadpoles at home as I have said, I was interested in gnats, I was interested in everything.

Because chemistry is at the heart of everything?

Yes, it seemed to me that it was, that's exactly how it seemed to me. Which is why I harboured a certain aversion to being taught Italian, which was so extraneous to me. Azelia Arici was a follower of Gentile and Croce,[45] she considered the natural sciences and physics and mathematics to be subsidiary subjects, ancillary, second-class. A debate which we took up again many years later after the war when we became friends and I went to visit her. She was very surprised by all that, it was a new world to her.

That is to say, your revelation of the hidden effects of her teaching?

Yes, of her teaching that I put up with. I wrote really bad essays, and so ... Yes, I enjoyed Dante and so I was able to find something to say about him, but Carducci, Pascoli and

---

[45] The ideas of the idealist philosophers Giovanni Gentile (1875–1944) and Benedetto Croce (1866–1952) played a major part in shaping the humanities-based school curriculum which Levi found so restrictive.

D'Annunzio really didn't interest me much, I endured them as a necessary evil. I have a different opinion of them now.

So, let's see. Do you think that the Gentile reform[46] effectively caused damage to your generation and to those that followed it?

I can't make the comparison but I would say that it did. And, among other things, it certainly deprived Italy of some potential physics and maths geniuses who were discouraged right from the start.

Do you know of others in your class in the same situation, who organized things for themselves and made a school for themselves outside school?

Yes, in my class there was a genius, not a potential genius but a real one, who was Ennio Artom, the brother of Emanuele.[47]

I remember a moving portrait of the Artom Family by Augusto Monti.

There were the two brothers and their father. Emanuele died as a partisan. Ennio was the younger, an extremely precocious young man, and so precociously anti-fascist

---

[46] For Giovanni Gentile's reform of the Italian education system, see Introduction, pp. viii–ix.
[47] Primo Levi recalls Emanuele Artom in an article published in the Turin newspaper *La Stampa* on 11 April 1984, on the occasion of the dedication to Artom of a park in Mirafiori. His admiration is direct and obvious: 'On September 8, 1943, the Nazis invaded northern Italy, and Emanuele didn't hesitate: though he had no military experience, and was a stranger to violence, he joined the partisans, in the mountains. He endured discomforts and dangers

that he could boast of having twice been sent into internal exile at the age of fourteen. When Mussolini came to Turin, the police turned up at his house and took him to Torre Pellice. At fourteen years old he was already considered to be an extremely dangerous individual.

Were you all fascinated by him?

He was a very reserved boy, but he had an undeniable appeal, the appeal of someone who has extremely clear ideas about everything. He was already a linguist by then, he was a friend and pupil of Benvenuto Terracini,[48] he knew Hebrew really well. He was a born linguist who at the same time had absorbed, from his home background too, an anti-fascism very different from mine: it was real militant anti-fascism. He inspired an instinctive respect in everyone.

with cheerful pride, he became quick and daring; in January 1944, he was the political representative for the Action Party in Val Pellice. He was captured in a roundup, tortured atrociously for days, and humiliated, but he found in his frail body the strength to be silent: he didn't name names. He died on April 7, racked by torture ...' ('A Park Dedicated to Emanuele Artom', trans. Alessandra and Francesco Bastagli, *The Complete Works of Primo Levi*, Vol. III, New York: Liveright, 2015, p. 2638.) Emanuele Artom's diary *Tre vite. Dall'ultimo '800 alla metà del '900* [Three Lives: From the Late Nineteenth Century to the Middle of the Twentieth] (1954) was republished in 2008 as *Diario di un partigiano ebreo* [The Diary of a Jewish Partisan]. Augusto Monti writes about the Artom family, the father Emilio, the elder brother Emanuele and the younger one Ennio, in *Torino falsa magra e altre pagine torinese* [Turin False and Slender and other Turinese pages], ed. G. Tesio, 2006. (GT)
[48] The Italian-Jewish philologist and literary critic Benvenuto Terracini (1886–1968) was an expert in Italian dialects, especially Piedmontese. He spent the years 1941–47 in Argentina as a refugee from Fascism before returning to take up the chair in linguistics at the University of Turin.

Were you a friend of his?

I didn't dare to be a friend of his, I thought he was too superior.

Did he have friends in your class?

No, no, he was a loner. What's more, he wasn't much to look at, he was a small, ugly boy with spectacles, extremely robust. But he was so at odds with the model of virility which Fascism had designed for the young people of that time as to be surrounded by a cautious air of privilege. He was top of the class by definition, and the top of the class is not much loved.

Is he the only one of your classmates that you remember?

The only one. All the others were colourless characters.

Have you seen any of them since?

A few of them, yes.

Is there any relationship between your own vocation as a chemist and etymologist – and hence a linguist – and Artom's?

Yes, there is. I liked grammar, both Greek and Latin. I couldn't say why, probably for scientific reasons, because grammar is a science while the cult of the classics is not, and these were questions which the school didn't really cover. All the same, I already had that rather dilettante interest of mine in questions about how things are phrased, in questions about Greek verbs, in the relationships between Greek words and English words and German words and

Italian words, but it was an interest which no one encouraged, an interest in a vacuum.

Perhaps because your teachers felt out of their depth?

Coccolo used to praise me for it, he called me the 'grammaticus', the latinist. He spotted, he detected in me that taste for etymology, but the teaching of the classical languages wasn't scientific in those days, I don't know what it's like now, but it wasn't scientific. You were told nothing about the reasons for things, for example the obvious relationship between Latin and Greek.

But you read the classics.

We were taught grammar as if it was a gift of God, an illumination come down from on high, a grammar devoid of reasons, and we read the classics.

However, you had a different vocation.

On account of which, in spite of myself, I had a good knowledge of grammar, both Latin and Greek. I got good marks for Latin and Greek, better than for Italian.

What were your grades?

At the *liceo?* They were between adequate and good, between seven and eight. I got good marks in the natural sciences and mathematics, in Italian I was usually adequate except when something fired my imagination. My grades culminated in that disaster I told you about, that three for Italian in my *liceo* leaving certificate. It was my first and only fail mark.[49]

---

[49] Carole Angier describes this incident in *The Double Bond: Primo Levi: A Biography* (London: Viking, 2002), pp. 103–5. 'Primo Levi,

What do you remember firing your imagination?

Ariosto, yes, Ariosto. I liked Ariosto.[50]

Characters on the move, captured, deserted, rescued, a really convoluted plot.

It touched my imagination. Those continual journeys, those impossible landscapes, idyllic, full of action. I also liked Ariosto's poetic technique, and Dante's as well. I really liked Dante's *Inferno*, *Purgatorio* not quite so much, and *Paradiso* I no longer remember.

Once again because the teachers weren't up to it?

Inferno is easy, it's in technicolor.

Theological notions?

Scientific ones as well.

who had never failed an academic subject in his life, whose most regular mark throughout school was eight out of ten, failed Italian, and had to retake all his examinations in October.' His classmate Fernanda Pivano, who had chosen the same essay subject, the Spanish Civil War, 'received the same mark as he: three out of ten' despite being 'a top student on the literary side'. Her failure was due to having written 'a romantically antifascist and antiwar essay, in which flowers had grown from the barrels of guns,' and she asked Levi whether he had done the same, to which he replied, 'Are you mad ... You know I'm Jewish.'

[50] Ludovico Ariosto's epic poem *Orlando Furioso*, composed between 1506 and 1532, is an action-packed and fantastical version of the French story of Roland.

When you reread Dante later on, did you have the same preferences?

I've reread the whole of *Purgatorio*, but not *Paradiso*. *Paradiso* puts me off. I never pick it up.

You've really never reread it?

No.

Have you kept your reports?

No, none of them.

Your leaving certificate?

Yes, I've kept that.

Did the fact of being Jewish weigh more heavily on you in liceo *than in elementary school or* ginnasio?

A little bit more in *liceo*, because of that friendship-antagonism that I described in 'A Long Duel'.[51] You know what I mean?

---

[51] Levi is alluding to 'A Long Duel' – included in *Other People's Trades*, trans. Raymond Rosenthal, London: Michael Joseph, pp. 52–58 – in which he tells of a contradictory and competitive friendship with a boy who in the story is called Guido, and who may correspond to the real-life Mario Losano. Giorgio Brandone mentions this in 'Primo Levi e il "D'Azeglio"' his valuable contribution to the conference on *I luoghi di Levi tra letteratura e memoria* [Primo Levi's places, literature and memory] held at the Liceo D'Azeglio in 2008. (GT)

Yes, when you talked about the race at the Stadium.

That was a really curious episode. This friend-enemy was intrigued by the fact that I was Jewish and needled and provoked me, and it also interested him. I still have the edition of Carducci's poems, a Zanichelli edition on India paper, on the cover of which he wrote 'Jew' in saliva, ruining the cover. It's still written there, you can still see it. Despite all that, I found myself paradoxically attracted by him, because of his disruptive vitality and his precocious sexuality which was beyond my experience. And besides, he stuck to me like a leech so that I would help him with his written work, I was a bit of a guide to him, a bit of a teacher. In exchange he taught me the paths by which you could get to the Sangone[52] on a bicycle, he challenged me to bicycle races. I saw him again during the war. During the war he was a soldier, he had been in Greece, and I said to him brutally that I hoped that Italy would lose the war and he replied, 'I can only forgive you because you are a Jew'. Since then I've heard nothing more of him, I've never seen his name anywhere, I don't know anything about him.

Have you never looked for him?

I've seen that he's in the telephone directory but I've never tried to get back in contact with him.

In any case, he was a Fascist while you were not.

He was effectively a Fascist, a follower of the cult of virility, but he was extremely cynical even when it came to

---

[52] The Sangone is a torrent river which rises 2,000 metres above sea level in the Cottian Alps and flows into the river Po.

Fascism. He believed in nothing, he was the prototype of a certain kind of Italian for whom physical strength and bodily vigour mattered a great deal. Doctrine didn't matter to him at all, he certainly wasn't a disciplined Fascist.

Did you become close to any of your other schoolmates apart from him? Anyone you used to see a bit more often, go to the cinema with perhaps?

Yes, I had a friend, we used to go to the cinema, we spent a great deal of time together and visited each other's houses by turns. I had, and indeed I still have, a friend from *liceo* with whom I always kept up a close and friendly relationship until he got married, but not afterwards.

Was it his marriage which broke the bond?

It was because I didn't know what to say to his wife. He had been a bachelor for a long time and as long as he was a bachelor we had a complete and genuine intimacy. Once he was married, that intimacy came to an end.

Jumping forward in time, did your own marriage change things too?[53]

That question is indeed a jump forward. My wife transformed everything, it was a dramatic event, and a marvellous one.

[53] In her biography of Levi, *The Double Bond* (op. cit., p. 476), Carole Angier, quoting 'his first biographer', Myriam Anissimov (*Primo Levi: Tragedy of an Optimist*, trans. Steve Cox, London: Aurum Press, 1998), writes that 'it is not possible to exaggerate what his marriage meant to Primo Levi. It meant [...] all he had longed for since the Lager, "an affirmation of the right, so fiercely denied him, to be a man".' (GT)

Going back to the subject of friendship. We mentioned the cinema. What did cinema mean to you?

French cinema meant a great deal to us, it represented something which was missing in Italy. Films made in Italy were anaemic.

The so-called 'white telephones'?[54]

Mino Doro,[55] Maria Denis ...[56] They didn't plumb the depths, but French films did. They showed life as it was, or at least how it seemed to be, even in its tragic implications. I'm talking of Renoir, of Jean Gabin, of *Le jour se lève*, *Carnet de bal*, *The Deserter*[57] (I don't recall its precise

[54] Italian film comedies made in the 1930s were referred to as *telefoni bianchi* [white telephone] movies because their Art Deco sets often included this status symbol, which signified wealth and glamour.

[55] Mino Doro (1903–2006) was a supporting and character actor who was portrayed in 1930s film magazines as an Italian Clark Gable. One of his roles was as a blackshirt in the 1934 Fascist propaganda film *Vecchia guardia* [The Old Guard].

[56] Maria Denis (Maria Esther Beomonte, 1916–2004) starred in *telefoni bianchi* films from 1936 to 1942, playing girl-next-door roles. In 1944 she was tried for collaboration on the grounds that she had been the mistress of Pietro Koch, the brutal Roman police chief during the Nazi occupation, though she claimed that she had in fact been making use of his infatuation with her to save the life of the film director Luchino Visconti, a claim which Visconti himself always refused to confirm.

[57] *Le jour se lève* [Daybreak] (1939) was directed by Marcel Carné and stars Jean Gabin as a foundry worker whose murder of a corrupt and manipulative rival in love leads to his death at the hands of the police. In *Carnet de bal* [Dance Programme] (1937), directed by Julien Duvivier, a widow sets out to explore her past by reconnecting with her former suitors. *Le Déserteur* [*The Deserter*] (1939), directed by Léonide Moguy, is an escapist version of the plot

Italian title). They arrived in Italy somewhat censored, but all the same the message got across. Sometimes we also used to go to the theatre, to see Govi[58] for instance, which was a very comforting bit of escapism. We instinctively felt that Govi was something authentic.

A subtle message which came from the everyday.

Yes, this man who was ordinary in every way, who expressed himself in a down-to-earth language, his Ligurian dialect. And we also used to go to the mountains and this was important. I have never been a great climber or a great skier, but we used to go to the mountains. This too was a way of removing oneself a little from the soporific atmosphere of Turin in those days. You could say that almost every Sunday in the winter we would go to the mountains, to the usual places: Bardonecchia, Sestriere, Claviere.[59] The Val D'Aosta was a bit too far away then.

How did you get there?

Coaches would be booked which took four hours to reach Sestriere, but the journey was entertaining in itself.

An early morning start?

Waking up at five.

---

of *Le jour se lève*: the deserter of the title jumps off a troop train in search of his sweetheart and successfully rejoins his regiment a couple of hours later having killed his wicked rival.
[58] The Italian actor and screenwriter Gilberto Govi (1885–1966) was the founder of the Genoese Dialectal Theatre.
[59] Sestiere and Claviere are Alpine ski resorts which, like Bardonecchia, lie to the west of Turin near the French border.

And with different companions from your schoolmates?

Usually with schoolmates, but sometimes we went with Fascist organizations, that is to say with the so-called alpine *avanguardisti*, but they never taught us anything, we were never taught to ski.

Was there somebody in charge?

There was a man who was supposed to teach us but he didn't know how to ski himself, so I never learnt.

Returning to the theatre and the cinema, which ones did you go to?

All of them from time to time, especially the cheapest ones. In those days, there were first run, second run and third run cinemas. We would wait until films were old enough to return for a second or third run.

Do you remember any cinemas in particular?

Yes, the one that is now called the Arlecchino, then it was called the Imperia and it cost a lira and eighteen cents, a lira and a soldo. There were cinemas that charged 80 cents.

Were there also cinemas of ill repute?

Yes, the Porta Nuova cinema, I think it was called.

It was still there in my day, the one under the Via Nizza arcade on the corner of Via Berthollet.

Yes, it was open in the morning, you could go there instead of going to school.

Did you ever play truant from school?

At the *liceo* no, but at university yes.

Never at the liceo, *but some of your schoolmates did.*

Some of them, yes, the most daring ones.

It wasn't really such a great transgression.

No

Did you smoke?

I started smoking after the war.

But did you never have the urge to try something transgressive, to do something which made you feel like a man?

My transgression was mountaineering. I started to do reckless things quite early on, at university, not at the *liceo*. That was my transgression.

You tested yourself against danger, you provoked it?

Yes.

But we have already reached the period of your friendship with Delmastro.[60] *But I have the impression that he acted more judiciously, he was more level-headed.*

He knew more than I did, but he loved danger too.

[60] Sandro Delmastro joined the Justice and Liberty anti-fascist resistance movement, and became the commanding officer for all their

66   The Last Interview

Sandro Delmastro was a friend from your university years ...

Yes.

Which liceo *had he been to?*

To the Alfieri.

What was his family background?

He came from a middle-class family. He was the son of a master mason.

He didn't come from an educated family. Did you perhaps represent the studious type to him?

I represented someone who took chemistry seriously.

Did any differences ever come between you?

Ah, it was pure admiration! That young man who was so taciturn, so sparing of words, so physically capable, sure of himself. He had a brother who was even better than he was, as he had an ugly face. His brother, as well as sharing all his good qualities, was extremely handsome, he was a Messner[61] in short. Without making any fuss about it,

operations in the city. Sent to the Val Roja after escaping from his first arrest, he was arrested again as he tried to reach his destination. Taken to the Fascist headquarters in Cuneo, he was killed during a desperate attempt to escape. The chapter 'Iron' in *The Periodic Table* is his literary transformation. (GT)

[61] Reinhold Messner, born in 1944, is an Italian mountaineer who in 1974 made the first ascent of Mount Everest without supplementary oxygen, and was also the first to climb all fourteen peaks over 8,000 metres above sea level.

they had done memorable things together, traversing the entire mountain arc around the Cogne basin[62] – with no break – without stopping. They were mentioned for it in the CAI bulletin,[63] but for them it was the victory in itself which counted, so they attached absolutely no importance to that.

It's hard to believe such characters could exist.

Characters out of Jack London. He barely told me about his exploits, just about bivouacs buried under the snow which he had dug, nights spent in the open in the middle of winter, bicycle rides all the way to Sestriere in order to go skiing, legendary stuff. He took me under his wing to teach me the essential things. I was physically very inferior to him.

Physically inferior but you made up for it with your agility.

I was certainly agile, and also determined.

What does it take to be a mountaineer?

It takes resistance to the cold and resistance to fatigue.

Was it the friendship of your life?

It had a fundamental effect on me for many years, which is fading only now. Our friendship involved sharing a little

---

[62] The alpine meadows of the Cogne Basin in the Val d'Aosta, at the heart of the Gran Paradiso National Park, are dominated by spectacular mountain ridges and peaks which are very popular with climbers.
[63] The Club Alpino Italiano [Italian Alpine Club].

of everything, we shared confidences, we shared mountaineering, we shared curiosity. And also concerts.

*Where? At the Conservatoire? But we were talking about
friendship ...*

Yes, friendship was very important and it still is, friendships between men and also with girls.

*So putting it all in order, let's see: mountaineering, the
cinema, concerts, the theatre. Was the theatre just for light
entertainment?*

No, not only that. Shakespeare as well. Whatever was on
offer, in short.

Did you go to the theatre often?

No, four or five times a year.

To the cinema?

Perhaps ten times a year.

Then you mentioned concerts.

The concerts for which I had a season ticket.

So you were able to go more frequently.

Yes.

So music is very important to you.

I have never played anything, so music was passive, a passive interest of mine, fascinating but passive. It has never entered my head to take lessons. I started to, my family tried to make me take piano lessons when I was six or seven years old, but I cried, I didn't want to do it, I lacked the application.

And you have never tried since. Is the same thing true of your sister?

Ah yes, just the same. She didn't do it either.

Your children?

My children are both exceptionally musical. Both of them can learn any instrument, they play together, they take courses. And my son, as a physicist, is also knowledgeable about the physics of music. My children are extremely musically gifted.

Memorable concerts?

None that I can think of.

Let's return for a little to friendship. Did you feel there was a difference between your friendships with men and with women?

Now you are touching on a very delicate matter, because I was shy, pathologically shy, so although I did have friendships with women, it stopped there. The transformation, the leap across the barricade, took place extremely late for me, after Auschwitz. It is a subject which I talk about with a certain discomfort, a certain difficulty. The fact is that I was inhibited, you can see it from my writing. I was extremely inhibited, also because of the racial campaign,[64] because it caused a definite breach. A lot of girls distanced themselves in the nicest possible way, without causing offence, but I sought out precisely the ones that it was impossible for me to have a relationship with.

You sought out the ones who rejected you?

Perhaps I did, but I leave that to others. In fact I did have a few friendships with girls, but none of them developed into love.

Not even with that university friend – you talked about her under a false name in The Periodic Table *– with whom you used to exchange books?*

Not even with her. That is to say, yes, I was slightly in love with her, but in an extremely chaste way.[65]

---

[64] The passing of the racial laws was preceded by the publication in July 1938 of the *Manifesto degli scienziati razzisti* [Manifesto of the Racial Scientists], which aped Nazi theories of race by declaring that Italians were Nordic Aryans and thus racially pure, while Jews and Africans were biologically inferior. This, together with a long anti-Semitic press campaign, paved the way for the oppressive legislation which followed.

[65] In the story 'Zinc' (the third chapter in *The Periodic Table*) this friend is called Rita, and Levi introduces her in this way: 'In one corner there was a hood, and Rita sat in front of it. I went over to her and realized with fleeting pleasure that she was cooking my same dish: with pleasure, I say, because for some time now I had been hanging around Rita, mentally preparing brilliant conversational openings, and then at the decisive moment I did not dare come out with them and put it off to the next day'. (*The Periodic Table*, op. cit., p. 34.) Carole Angier, in her biography *The Double Bond* (op. cit., pp. 124–5), has identified Clara Moschino under the name and character of Rita. (GT)

And did all this make you suffer?

Yes, it made me suffer terribly, I suffered in an appalling way, because I saw all of my friends having this kind of experience, including sexual experience. But I didn't, and it made me suffer in a dreadful way, to the point of considering suicide.

Perhaps also because you had male friends who showed off about their conquests a bit too much ...

Yes indeed. One of them went to a brothel, he went with a false identity card. I would never have done a thing like that.

Friendships with women which have stood the test of time?

Oh, quite a few, yes, quite a few. For instance, there was my friendship with that girl in 'Phosphorus' in *The Periodic Table*. She is still a friend of mine.[66] But the last two or three years have really been a period when friendships have broken up.

Why?

For various reasons. To start with, because of my own situation, family circumstances on account of which I don't get out much, and then ... some people have died, some have fallen ill, some have lost their interest in life ... It's a chapter which is coming to an end.

[66] The girl in the story 'Phosphorus' is a literary version of Gabriella Garda; see pp. 205–9 of Carole Angier's *The Double Bond* (op. cit.). (GT)

Is that how it feels to grow old?

Yes.

Seeing your social circle crumble around you?

Yes, and this is very distressing, very distressing and irreversible.

But all in all, do you regard yourself as someone with a positive nature?

Well, I consider myself to be someone who has fought quite a few battles. Who has lost some and won others. I must have a certain deep-down strength because I survived Auschwitz, and that was a very great battle. As a chemist too I have suffered some defeats, but I have won quite a lot of the time. Then, as a writer. I found myself becoming a writer almost in spite of myself, I started a new chapter. I have been gradually overwhelmed, first in Italy and then abroad, by this wave of success which has profoundly affected my equilibrium and put me in the shoes of someone I am not.

Is being a writer the heaviest job?

The heaviest?

Yes, that was the question.

In terms of its consequences, undoubtedly yes. In terms of time and effort, I would say not, because I have generally written my books freely and easily without finding that it weighed on me.

Have you never felt the weight of a possible defeat, that is to say of not being able to do it? In short, how do you feel about such an elusive business as writing? An obligation to write? A need to do it?

That is a weight I feel now, but not earlier. I've always felt quite self-confident as a writer, also because the critics supported me and I used to read things to my friends who praised me for them, because the sales were good and my publisher was happy. I have hardly ever felt like a struggling writer, on the contrary I am still very surprised by the fact that I succeeded, that I was able to do it without even having to sweat over it.

Like a fact of nature ...

It's a phenomenon which takes place outside of me. I write a book and then the book takes its own path, it sets off on complicated, labyrinthine journeys. *If This is a Man* has had such a complicated journey that I'm unable to follow it and it's still going on today. It's been reprinted in Germany, and only this morning I was phoned by a film technician, a scriptwriter, with a proposal to make it into a film.

However, from what you said earlier, one could say that this new profession changed something for you, and inside you. Haven't you said yourself that you felt like a man with two faces, at least while you were carrying on your two professions?

Yes indeed.

And did this not create psychological problems, didn't it cause ambiguity?

Not ambiguity, hybridism. I carried it off well, I coped with it really well, I have to say that I was up to the task for quite a few years.

How did you manage practically speaking?

I divided my time in two: there was my time in the factory, which had nothing to do with literature, and then the time after: answering letters, evenings spent writing.

Did you work an eight-hour day in the factory?

Yes, plus two hours of travel, which makes ten. I used to work at night. I'm very strong, that's all there is to it.

No moments of weakness?

Yes, like the one I told you about just now. But not as far as writing is concerned. I've had some to do with my work in the factory, I've had some weak moments in that regard, yes.

In any case, they didn't concern your writing?

No.

So that's something positive, isn't it?

Not what I've already written, but the process of writing, yes. Right now, for instance, I'm incapable of writing, but I don't reject the things I have written, they are my own flesh and blood.

Leaving aside your present situation, you have always found, as a writer, that you could control the situation.

I have had some difficult times, I've had them often, I've often been seized by ... but I would prefer not to go into that.

But when you are faced by those difficult times, how do you react?

I try to combat them with the means at my disposal, but ... But in any case, the fact that you are questioning me about these things while I find myself in crisis makes me see things in a different light. At a different time I would reply in a different way, I would talk about it with much more enthusiasm.

I understand, but I can't fail to observe that you have always conquered the beast.

Right now, that means nothing to me. I've told you from the start that these are confessions which will need to be translated.

I'm well aware that you are saying things to me that you might not say at a different time, but is that not also to some extent the measure of a conversation which plumbs the depths?

I live in suspicion[67] because of this inhibition of mine which I told you about, and which poisoned the years

---

[67] Levi is quoting from the medieval Florentine poet Fazio degli Uberti (1305–1367), whose sonnet on avarice, based on Dante's image of the wolf in *Inferno* canto I, reads like a subjective

of my youth and still cuts me off from certain human relationships.

But you see, and I say this with the greatest respect, there are times when this limitation is evident in your writing. As if there was a sort of barrier beyond which you are unable to go.

I don't want to go beyond it.

I'll put it in a less indirect way: as if you lacked warmth.

I don't know, I'm not really aware of that.

A sort of holding back ...

That's certainly true. There is a trace of it – I can also tell you – in the opening pages of *If This is a Man*, an allusion to a woman. I courted that woman in my own fashion, causing her great embarrassment, because she was aware of my extreme shyness and indecision. We were taken prisoner together, in what was actually quite a banal way. We were in hiding in the Col de Joux[68] and we had gone down into the valley on I don't know what political mission and

---

description of clinical depression: 'quanto più di vita ho lungo spazio/ più moltiplica in me questa tristizia./ Io vivo con sospetto e con malizia,/ né lemosina fo, né Dio ringrazio./ Deh odi s'io mi vendo e s'io mi strazio.' [the longer that my lifetime stretches out/ the more this anguish multiplies in me./ I live in suspicion and malevolence/ nor give alms to my neighbour, nor thank God./ Ah, think if I sell and lacerate myself.] (Fazio Degli Uberti, 'Avarice', *Rime*, ed. Giuseppe Corso, *Scrittori d'Italia*, Vol. 207, Bari: Laterza, 1952, p. 49.)

[68] A high mountain pass in the French alps, bordering the Italian Val d'Aosta.

we were offered shelter there so that we wouldn't have to climb back up at night. We refused, I can't really remember why, and climbed back up to the Col de Joux that night, and five hours later, a night later, we were arrested and I have often felt guilty about it.

For having involuntarily helped to cause your arrest?

What's more, this woman attempted suicide in order not to be deported, she cut her veins, but they were stitched up again. In short, I carried the burden of her death – because she did die – until I met my present wife. It was a really desperate situation for me, being in love with someone who was gone and, what's more, whose death one had caused, and I think that what one feels is ... Perhaps if I had been less inhibited with her, if we had run away together, if we had made love ... I was incapable of those things.[69]

It's an old story now. Have you ever thought of writing your autobiography?

I have written it.

---

[69] Already close to Levi during his time working for Wander (the pharmaceutical company which he joined on moving to Milan, after his semi-clandestine job in the asbestos quarry in Balangero), Vanda Maestro was one of the seven 'friends from Turin, boys and girls', of whom Levi gives a disguised account in 'Gold' (*The Periodic Table*, op. cit., pp. 127–8): 'Vanda was a chemist like me but could not find a job, and was permanently irritated by this because she was a feminist'. They met again in the Val d'Aosta during his time as an unprepared partisan, and then in the Fossoli camp. Vanda died in the Lager, which was for Levi – who had fallen in love with her – a constant anguish, as he confesses in the opening pages of *If This is a Man*, then again in *The Truce*, and also here in this interview, in a far more harrowing confession. (GT)

But I don't mean The Periodic Table, *which is only an autobiography in a manner of speaking. I mean an explicit autobiography, without any filter other than the writing itself. Talking, for instance, about the setbacks of a profession is a different matter from talking about the setbacks of a life in the deepest sense.*

In truth it would be too painful for me.

That was the sense of my question.

As I have said, I went through a decidedly unhappy adolescence and youth because of my inability to establish a solid romantic relationship with a girl ... but these are not things which should be talked about.

I understand. In any case, the best part of your life came later. Your return, your marriage, your children, your books, your writing with its therapeutic potential. Writing was also to some extent a healing process ...

Yes it was, but *If This is a Man* is very dramatic, as I have said. Those two convergent facts, of starting to write *If This is a Man* and meeting the woman who is now my wife, were the two factors of my salvation.

The meeting with your wife, for instance, could you tell me about that?

Certainly, I should like to tell you. I would say it was a question of seconds rather than minutes. I already knew her, she was a friend of my sister.

You knew her before your deportation?

Yes, before my deportation, one of my sister's many girl-friends. We went dancing together and, in the course of a few seconds, we were aware of a profound and unexpected change, the disappearance of that barrier of inhibition, thanks above all to her, who made me talk, who was patient with me, was understanding, was loving and in the course of a few minutes ...

Where did you go to dance? Do you remember?

I no longer remember that, probably to the Jewish school.

Do you remember the date?

Yes, there is a poem in *At an Uncertain Hour* which is the one that I wrote on that occasion. Do you remember it?[70]

Perhaps the one in which you talk about the stars and God's mistake ...

Yes, the date is that of the poem I mentioned.

Was it in the evening or during the day?

In the evening, yes.

And it was a sudden and overwhelming thing.

Yes, sudden and overwhelming.

---

[70] The poem, included in *At an Uncertain Hour*, is called '11 February 1946' (Primo Levi, *Collected Poems*, op. cit., p. 16). (GT)

So that you felt as if there was a before and an after.

As I relate in the chapter 'Chromium' in *The Periodic Table*.

And it made you euphoric.

It made me euphoric, fulfilled, free and happy, full of the desire to work, a double victory, I felt I was the master of the world.

We've jumped forward in time. Shall we go back a little, to the university stage of your studies, to the time when you enrolled.

I had no hesitations. I had had that setback, failing the *liceo* leaving certificate which I then retook in October with coaching from Umberto Cosmo.

You went to Cosmo. What impression did he make on you as a private tutor?

Poor thing, he was very embarrassed.

Did you go to his house, in Corso Mediterraneo?

In Via Colli.

Yes, his daughter still lives there. How old was he then?

I don't know, sixty-five? He seemed very old to me.

And who sent you to him?

Azelia Arici herself. No, no, it can't have been her, because I would have to write an essay on a Fascist subject. I don't remember which friend sent me to Cosmo. He gave me some good advice, he made me do some exercises. I got through in October, but I don't remember with what grade.

Don't you even remember the subject of the essay?

No.

And then?

Then I immediately enrolled at the university and I enjoyed it very much. I really enjoyed the atmosphere, I enjoyed the course, I enjoyed the textbooks, I was in my element.

And were your professors up to the mark?

Yes, I had a high opinion of almost all my professors and they thought the same about me, but a year later the racial laws were passed. We've reached '38–'39.

And at that point you had to …

No, the law allowed me to continue my studies, fortunately for me, and to start with I felt different, though I was not the only Jew, there were quite a few of us. There were seven or eight of us out of an intake of about sixty, and I must say that both our professors and our fellow students behaved like gentlemen, they did not make us feel it or let it weigh on us at all …

Not at all?

When it was a question of the graduation thesis, yes, because it was forbidden to accept us as internal students, as it was called then. And some of them said brutally,

'You're a Jew so I can't accept you'. Others said it in a nicer way and one of them accepted me illicitly.

In what sense? In the sense that legally speaking you were off the record?

I was off the record, I simply wasn't there. So I ended up writing a subsidiary dissertation[71] on physics which was longer than my thesis itself because I also did some experimental research.

Have you kept your university record book? Did you have to take a lot of exams?

Twenty-five.

Did you get through them without any problems?

With those exams? No, none.

Nothing, in other words, that you didn't like.

Well, I liked some things more and others less. The chemistry of building materials didn't interest me very much. I was attracted to theoretical chemistry and to experimental chemistry too.

---

[71] The thesis which formed the final part of Levi's undergraduate degree course had to be accompanied by a subsidiary dissertation. As Levi relates in the 'Potassium' chapter of *The Periodic Table*, he wrote his subsidiary dissertation on physics rather than chemistry partly because the only one of his university teachers willing to take him on as a supervisee was the young physics lecturer Nicolò Dallaporta.

Was the fact that you didn't stay in that environment due to your being a Jew?

In the university environment? Well, afterwards I found a job as a matter of urgency, because my father was very ill, and I took the one I found in Balangero[72] and after that with Wander.

Your father?

My father had had an intestinal tumour in '35, which had been operated on, but he had a metastatic growth in '42.

While you were still at university?

In '42 I had already left. I graduated in July '41.

Your thesis?

My thesis properly speaking I wrote on stereochemistry[73] with Professor Ponzio.[74]

---

[72] The Poggio San Vittore asbestos mine, where Levi found a job, was in the municipal territory of Balangero, a town about twenty-five kilometres northwest of Turin.
[73] Stereochemistry is a branch of chemistry concerned with the effects on chemical reactions of the three-dimensional arrangement of atoms and molecules. Levi's degree thesis involved looking at asymmetry in carbon molecules, a phenomenon which was first observed by the Latvian chemist Paul Walden (1863–1957) in 1896. It is no accident that the key element in the famous chapter which ends *The Periodic Table* is carbon.
[74] The title of the thesis was *The Walden Inversion*. Giacomo Ponzio (1870–1945) was the head of general and inorganic chemistry from 1915 to 1941 at the University of Turin, where he was also the director of the Institute of General Chemistry. (GT)

Did he chose your thesis topic?

I chose it myself.

What particularly attracted you to it?

Stereochemistry itself, that is to say the chemistry of molecules regarded as solid bodies with their own structures and internal dynamics. I should say that it was an intelligent thesis, in fact I was awarded distinction. My subsidiary dissertation was in experimental physics, as I've already told you.

Did you have a high opinion of Professor Ponzio? Or did you choose him as your supervisor because he was the most willing to take you on?

No, no. I chose my thesis topic because the subject interested me and he agreed to that right away. He was very intelligent. I remember the exact words he said to me: 'You are a very distinguished student, but I can't accept you.' On account of the racial laws.

So then, if it had not been for the racial laws, you could have stayed at the university.

I would certainly have had a university career.

Were the university premises those on Corso Massimo d'Azeglio?

Yes.

The ones with the minaret?

The minaret isn't there any more. They demolished it. There is still one left, the physiology one, but the chemistry one has been demolished. The minaret was actually a combustion chimney.

And how do you remember the Turin of those days?

That's rather hard to say. I don't remember it all that well. Certainly it was easier to walk than it is now, and it was also more pleasant to walk, there weren't all these cars.

But have you never lived in this city while wishing to be somewhere else, to make a complete change?

They were only ever qualified thoughts of escape. That is to say, I wanted to travel but then to come back here.

Could one say that you are a stay-at-home?

Yes, I'm a stay-at-home.

After all this time we haven't yet dealt with the subject of reading.

From *liceo* onwards? You have my anthology, *The Search for Roots* ... there's not much more to add. Well, my father brought home piles of books. Céline, for example, Dos Passos ...

Céline? Did you say Céline?[75]

Céline, yes.

[75] The French novelist Louis-Ferdinand Céline (the pen name of Louis Ferdinand Auguste Destouches, 1894–1961) is best known

Céline is very hard-hitting, don't you think?

I don't like that style of writing, I find it disordered and anarchic, however I have read him. *The Magic Mountain* ...[76]

That's a different matter.

I liked that very much.

Because you were struck by the theme of illness, TB, the sanatorium?

Neither yes nor no. I was interested in the metaphysical discussions, the discussions between Naphtha and Settembrini. I was interested in the atmosphere, I was interested in the characters, I didn't pay much attention to the theme of illness.

What kind of reader are you?

A microscopically close one, I'm interested in the structure of a sentence. That passion for grammar which I told you about.

for his nihilistic and iconoclastic first novel, *Journey to the End of the Night*, and for the virulently anti-Semitic pamphlets he produced between 1937 and 1941.
[76] In the 'Zinc' chapter of *The Periodic* Table, Levi is delighted to discover that Rita (the real-life Clara Moschino) is also reading Thomas Mann's great novel: 'it was my sustenance during those months, the timeless story of Hans Castorp in enchanted exile on the magic mountain' (op. cit., p. 35).

It seems to me that all this fits with your 'restrained' style. I think that one could, for instance, make a study of your relative clauses.

That might be interesting.

Going back to Mann and The Magic Mountain, *that was definitely something you read at university.*

At university, yes. Other writers, such as Dos Passos and Faulkner, I'm not sure about.

Did Vittorini or Pavese come into this?

No, I read them in the Dall'Oglio editions, I think.

Pavese and Vittorini?

I didn't have anything by Vittorini or by Pavese either.

Later discoveries?

Yes.

So which writers do you remember?

Well, I also read a lot of rubbish. I read Sholem Asch[77] and Jack London, Kipling. They were almost required reading.

---

[77] Sholem Asch (1880–1957) was a Polish-Jewish novelist and play-wright who emigrated to the United States in 1910 but continued to write in Yiddish, portraying Jewish life both in the Polish shtetl and in the immigrant community of the Lower East Side of New York.

Also Guido da Verona? And Pitigrilli?[78]

No, my father wasn't happy to have books of that kind in the house.

Verne?

Verne, of course.

Not Salgari.

Not Salgari. I did actually read one book by Salgari, but it didn't have much to say to me.

No forbidden books?

No. I didn't buy my own books, my father bought them.

---

[78] Guido da Verona (1881–1939) and Pitigrilli, the pseudonym of Dino Segre (1893–1975), were two popular writers whose combination of eroticism and humour meant that they enjoyed great success with the public in the period between the two world wars. (GT)

Sunday, 8 February

Where had we got to?

To your time at university or just afterwards.

I can't remember what we've already talked about and what I haven't told you yet.

It doesn't matter. We'll be able to go back over it.

My story began immediately after I graduated. I really needed to start earning because my father was very ill and we had the really crazy idea of setting up our own laboratory.

Which you talk about in The Periodic Table.

No, I don't think I talked about that.

I thought that in 'Arsenic', when you talk about the cobbler and the analysis he wanted done, wasn't that in your own laboratory?

Yes, but this was a previous one, this happened earlier. With the same person, with the same friend Emilio from *The Periodic Table.*

May I know his real name?

Yes, he's called Alberto Salmoni,[79] and his father did indeed have a monopoly of the blood from the abattoir in Corso Inghilterra[80] and he had some premises there in which we thought we could set ourselves up.

In Corso Inghilterra?

Yes, where the Sip[81] is now, there used to be an abattoir.

The old slaughterhouse.

Yes. We set up our own laboratory to mass-produce titration reagents, something which has later been done by other people. It was a crazy idea with the means at our disposal, we had no money.

---

[79] Alberto Salmoni is the real name of the character who is called Emilio in the story 'Tin' in *The Periodic Table.* There are some positively enamoured pages about him by Carole Angier in her biography, *The Double Bond.* (GT)

[80] Levi explains in *The Periodic Table* that 'the blood was turned into buttons, glue, fritters, blood sausages, wall paints and polishing paste' (op. cit., p. 186).

[81] The Società Italiana per l'Esercizio Telefonico, known as Sip, was the state monopoly telephone company from 1964 to 1994.

What are titration reagents?

They are phials containing an exact quantity, accurately weighed, of sulphuric acid for example, or caustic soda, or permanganate, and so on.

To be used for different things?

For analysis, to be used in other laboratories, to be used for titration,[82] which means establishing the concentration of other substances. But the business only lasted for a very short time ...

Was Alberto Salmoni – excuse the occasional interruption – a classmate of yours?

Yes, he was a classmate of mine, we took the same course, and that course has been a long one because he is still my friend today.

Did you meet at university or at the D'Azeglio?

We met on a coach coming back from Sestriere, where there was a very good-looking boy who sang really well, and later I discovered that that was him. But I didn't know he was Jewish. On more careful consideration, it becomes clear that it has something to do with *shalom*, which essentially means peace, it means Salomon,[83] it's

[82] Titration, also known as volumetric analysis, is used to measure the volume of a solution of the substance to be tested which exactly reacts with a solution of the reagent, thus determining the concentration of the former.
[83] Salomon, or Salomone, is the Italian form of the Biblical name Solomon, which, as Levi suggests, is derived from the Hebrew word *shalom*: peace.

a contraction of the name Salomon. I didn't know he was a Jew, there was nothing Jewish about his physical type or his way of behaving. He was a good-looking boy and he's still a good-looking man, and so – to digress – when the racial laws were passed he asked me, 'And you, how are you dealing with it?' I was very annoyed because I thought it was an impertinent question: 'I can deal with it. You Aryans can look after yourselves.' And he told me, 'No, I'm Jewish too.' Well, that laboratory only lasted for a short time because I received the offer of a job in Balangero, the one that I wrote about in 'Nickel'.

Was it only an idea or did you really set up the laboratory?

No, we really rigged it up in a rudimentary and risky way inside the abattoir. It was an utterly revolting place.

And how long did it last?

It lasted for a month perhaps.

So for a very short time. Can you tell me exactly which year this was?

The autumn of my graduation year, so it was in '41.

Revolting, you said?

Yes, especially that section. The whole of the abattoir was revolting, but especially that section because it was full of blood, coagulated blood. I talked about that in 'Tin' in *The Periodic Table*, when I was describing Alberto's father. He took his son under his wing and generously allowed us to use part of those premises.

What did he do later on?

The father?

No, Alberto Salmoni.

He changed his job a number of times. Now he doesn't do anything any more, that is to say he still owns a stationer's shop but he's actually retired now.

So this was the first project you carried out, even if only for a very short time.

Yes.

Have you ever fantasized about doing something else, did you already have other ideas in your head?

Well, I thought that one thing leads to another, so let's start by setting up a little laboratory and then see what we can do, if not what I told you about, that is to say reagents for analysis, then making preparations under contract. During the war, you found that kind of thing. Many raw materials were in short supply so there was the chance to make synthetic ones, as in fact we did immediately after the war.

Did you ever think of setting up a more ambitious enterprise?

Well, under those conditions, with the war going on, and the racial laws in place, it was a survival economy, you lived from day to day. The more far-sighted thought that things were going to go badly for the Jews whatever happened, whether the Germans were defeated or victorious. We were in serious trouble, so we were living in an extremely precarious situation.

Which didn't permit either projects or dreams.

No, projects were not possible. There was a feeling of tragedy in the air, although nobody knew yet what the tragedy would be, I didn't know how things would turn out. But all the same, after that brief interlude, things weren't too bad for me in Balangero, indeed I was quite all right there because I enjoyed the work.

The Balangero job offer, who did that come from?

From Ennio Mariotti,[84] he passed away five or six years ago.

Who was he, what did he do?

He was an army lieutenant, from an anti-fascist family. His father had exchanged gunshots with the Fascists in Florence. He was a Florentine, he was a very intelligent and very energetic man who was doing his military service with great repugnance, and his attitude to me was very authoritarian. So much so that mine was almost a rebellion. I found 'my' way of isolating the nickel and he really took umbrage at that, also because I was sent, following this, shall we say, little discovery of mine to Genoa, in fact to Cornigliano,[85] where there was a military laboratory, still

---

[84] In the story 'Nickel' in *The Periodic Table* he appears under the name of 'the lieutenant'. He died in 1982, so five years before our conversation. (GT)

[85] Cornigliano is a western quarter of Genoa.

in a semi-clandestine way because of the fact that I was Jewish, to test out other ways of enriching this material, and to perfect the method and so on.

How long were you there?

I stayed in Cornigliano for about two months and I took out a patent in my own name, something which wasn't really correct, but – as I told you – those were tragic years and I thought: having a patent in my own name is a qualification which could be useful, for instance if I have to escape to Switzerland or to some other place.

And did you live in Cornigliano?

I lived in Genoa, I had some relatives in Genoa, and I worked in Cornigliano.

So you lived there for a period which coincided with your Balangero job.

At the end of it, after Balangero.

So had your connection with Balangero already ended?

No, the assignment was for Balangero.

And after that?

Then I returned to Balangero and the story of the nickel came to an end. As I have recounted, there was nickel in greater quantities elsewhere and it wasn't worthwhile to continue the research. Incidentally, the story isn't really over. Depending on the market for nickel, there are still those who go to dig in Balangero and try ingenious methods to extract nickel from this very poor material.[86]

Successfully?

Not so far.

Clandestinely?

Clandestinely. They're amateurs, small-time chemists. Big business has never got involved with it as far as I know, but it's attractive because the material has already been crushed up, so the bulk of the work of grinding it has already been done.

And in your opinion, could this research still bear fruit today?

It all depends on the international price of nickel. If there was a boom in nickel it might be worth doing, having another go at it.

Is it all based on the unpredictability of the market or is there already an ongoing trend?

Impossible to tell. I hear from time to time that someone might want to come and talk to me about reviving that old idea I have described. It's still not completely dead.

---

[86] Since the material in question was the spoil from an asbestos mine, this was a risky as well as an unrewarding form of treasure hunting.

Shall we go back to Ennio Mariotti?

Yes, well you see he took it as an impropriety on my part
that I had taken out the patent in my own name and not
on behalf of the Balangero mine.

But you had patented it in your own name?

Yes, I had.

How long did the Balangero episode last?

It lasted about six months.

*Did you have any other relationships there that you par-
ticularly remember?*

Also with the manager, I remember him very well. He was
young, very energetic, just married to a white woman from
Tunisia, a French Tunisian, and he was very affectionate to
me and understood my situation, especially after the death
of my father which happened while I was in Balangero in
March '42. He used to invite me to play chess at his house.
We were quite good friends, in short.

*To digress for a moment. When did you start playing
chess?*

Oh, a very long time ago, with my father. My father
taught me. To begin with he used to win, then I began
to win, as tends to happen. Not because I played better
than him, but because my age meant I had more concentration and a better memory ... Just as my son beats me
now.

What was the manager called?

Marchioli.

Do you remember his first name?

No.

Is he someone it would be possible to get in touch with?

No, he died a few years ago too.

Did he live in Turin?

No, he always lived in Balangero and became general manager of the mine. No, he wasn't still in Balangero, he went to Ispra, I don't remember why.

In any case, you lived there in a semi-clandestine way?

Yes.

And what did that involve? Did you live there, did you have your own room?

Yes, I had a small room, I used to eat with a family of workers, all very nice people.

Who knew about your situation?

They had guessed it.

Without needing to talk about it?

As I wrote in *The Periodic Table*, I actually had a girl assistant who was the daughter of a Fascist *gerarca*. The *gerarca* himself invited me to lunch.

Something which could only happen here?

In Italy in general and particularly in the San Vittore mine, because it was a kind of republic, it was in an isolated place five kilometres from the plain.

A fascinating place too, I remember seeing it on the right when I was going to Lanzo.

Yes, it was also a fascinating place. Now it's no longer the same, now the wall of the cone-shaped crater that I described has been broken down and isn't there any more. There is just a vast plateau and since in the intervening period it has been possible to establish that asbestos is toxic, or at any rate hazardous, all the work is automated, it has changed completely.

So much so that – you told me – when the BBC came they raised difficulties because they didn't want to go there.

Yes.

One can't say, however, that you made genuine friendships there.

Not friendships, no, I didn't want to.

Was that due to the clandestine conditions?

In any case, friendships with whom? I was the only chemist. Lieutenant Mariotti came up there once a week, I was quite isolated.

Was the mine under the control of the army?

The mine was under the control of an organization called Cogefag, the Comissariato generale per le fabbricazioni di guerra.[87] Asbestos was considered to be a material of strategic interest, a war material, so there was a military inspector who came up every now and then and did nobody any harm.

This lasted for six months, you said?

Yes, from January to July '42, including the two months in Cornigliano, but perhaps it wasn't two, perhaps it was just one.

And then?

Then I had a phone call from Milan. Two things. Firstly, as I told you, the story of the nickel had come to an end, though they offered me the chance to stay there and work on other things, but I had had this offer from Milan, which was from Wander, that firm which makes Ovomaltina,[88] and I accepted it right away, also because I had relatives in Milan who would put me up.

Hence your poem 'Crescenzago'.[89] Can we piece together the make-up of the group? I know they were all the same age.

Yes, more or less the same age. There was a cousin of mine, more precisely a cousin of my mother's, who lived with her own mother in the centre of Milan and rented me a room.

---

[87] General Commissariat for War Production.
[88] The malted milk drink known as Ovaltine in the English-speaking world.
[89] *Collected Poems*, op. cit., p. 3. Crescenzago, described in Levi's poem as a place where exploited and exhausted workers breathe polluted air, is the district of Milan where the Ovomaltina factory was situated.

And you travelled from Milan to Crescenzago?

I travelled by tram or by bicycle from Milan to Crescenzago.

What memories do you have of that period?

Very good ones, they were extremely fruitful years. There were seven of us friends.[90]

Could you list them for me?

I can list them, certainly: Carla Consonni, Silvio Ortona, Emilio Diena, the architect Eugenio Gentili, that Vanda Maestro who was deported with me and died, the girl to whom I allude vaguely in *If This is a Man*, the cousin with whom I was staying, who died from Alzheimer's disease last year, and then there was me, which makes seven. And we spent happy evenings singing together, all kinds of different songs, organizing clandestine dinners with provisions from the black market.

What kind of a singer are you?

Terrible.

But you do sing if the occasion calls for it?

Yes, I used to sing. We had a repertoire, we would spend the evening singing.

---

[90] These were the seven friends from Turin that Levi talks about in the story 'Gold' in *The Periodic Table*. The complex relationships between them have been pieced together in all three of the biographies (by Ian Thomson, Myriam Anissimov and Carole Angier) so far dedicated to Primo Levi. (GT)

A repertoire of what kind?

Waldensian songs, Jewish songs, French songs.

Can you give me some examples?

Especially songs from the mountains, I could mention plenty of examples. But not give a demonstration.

I'm not asking you to sing them.

They don't have titles.

The first lines of some of them?

Il n'avait qu'une fille, Enfants de la mort laissez-vous conduire. They were French songs, because Silvio Ortona had a lot of French friends and they had taught him these French songs.

Who was the leader of the group?

I would say that it was a tie between Silvio Ortona and me. Silvio Ortona was more politically mature than me, I was more versatile and during that period I also wrote something which I have never owned up to. I wrote a story, which was never finished, about a man who lived outside time, found his way into time, was swept away by time. I've kept it, but it is unpublished and will stay unpublished.

How long is it?

Twenty pages.

Have you never thought about taking it up again?

No, it's a really juvenile story, it's contrived. It isn't badly written, it's contrived.

It doesn't feel yours, in short; it doesn't satisfy you stylistically.

No, it was influenced by the time of *The Magic Mountain*, influenced by the mountains, because at that time, haven't I told you? we were crazy about mountaineering, all of us including the girls. We used to do terrifying things ...

From Milan where did you go?

From Milan we cycled to the Grigna[91] on Saturday evenings.

Yes, you have told me.

It is fifty kilometres. We would set off as if it was nothing on Saturday evenings as far as Ballabio, I think, and then climb up to the Carlo Porta shelter-hotel.[92] We would sleep in the shelter and then the next day we would climb the Grigna peaks, which are demanding. I have a hole in my head which you can still feel.

---

[91] The Grigna is a mountain massif which rises above Lake Como in the Bergamo Alps. Its two peaks, Grignone and Grignetta, are popular with hikers and climbers.

[92] While some of the Italian *rifugi* [mountain shelters] offering food and basic accommodation to climbers are no more than huts, the Rifugio Carlo Porta, set up in 1911 by members of the Milan branch of the Italian Alpine Club, is a substantial building set in beautiful surroundings and offering easy access to the peaks and mountain walks of the Grigna.

May I touch it?

Can you feel that there's a dent in the cranium? It is where a stone was dropped onto my head.

You mean by someone you were ...

Another roped party of climbers, it was another party who dropped a stone onto me which nearly shattered my skull.

Perhaps you've already told me about that. That you then had to patch yourself up in a makeshift way because the wound was bleeding so much.

It bled a great deal, perhaps I've told you. The blood soaked into my clothes and came out of my trousers, it bled so much. But I cycled back to Milan all the same, I staunched the bleeding as best I could. It's odd, but in a single twenty-four hours, a Saturday and Sunday, I got all the scars that I have. This one that you can see, this callus here ... Because in order to go up to Ballabio I had put a fixed gear onto my bicycle which was very stiff and I was pedalling with that stiff gear. Then a van came past and I hung on to the van, forgetting that the pedals were still going round. I was thrown off the bicycle and ended up against a wall and I tore the whole length of my thumb. The next day the business with the stone happened.

You were a bit reckless, though.

Yes, I was a bit reckless.

As you've told me, you used to do some foolhardy things.

Yes, I used to do some foolhardy things.

But did leadership and recklessness help you to overcome your shyness or not?

To a certain extent yes, but only to a certain extent, because my shyness with girls was still there, and went on. Yes, there was a timid flirtation between me and Vanda Maestro, which led to our being captured together, which I have already told you about.

But in any case they were sustaining years.

Sustaining years too because they included the 25th of July, they included Badoglio.[93] On the 25th of July, everyone chose a path for themselves. I have to say that I knew very little about politics and I still don't know much, I have no gift for politics, but I opted for the Action Party and considered myself to be a member of the Action Party.[94] There was no membership strictly speaking, I distributed leaflets ...

[93] On 25 July 1943, following Mussolini's fall from power, Marshall Pietro Badoglio (1871–1956) took over the government of Italy. Instead of signing an immediate armistice with the Allies, who had landed in Sicily on 10 July, he initially declared that 'the war goes on'. The eventual armistice, which was secretly signed on his behalf on 3 September, was in fact an abject surrender, and its announcement by the Allies on 8 September immediately led to the German invasion of the north of Italy.

[94] 'Formed in the Summer of 1942, already defunct by 1946, the Action Party (*Partito d'Azione*), despite its short life span, left a strong and lasting mark on Italian intellectual and political life.' Like the Justice and Liberty (*Giustizia e libertà*) group which preceded it, the Action Party attempted to 'synthesize the best of Liberal and Socialist political cultures' into an effective anti-fascist force but 'ended up by disgruntling both.' (David Ward, *Antifascisms: Cultural Politics in Italy, 1943–46*, Madison, NJ: Fairleigh Dickinson University Press, 1996, pp. 124–6.) However, after the German invasion in September 1943, both groups, along with the Communists, played their part in the Italian resistance movement.

As a party it was born later.

Yes, later it was born as a party.

And it died too very soon.

Yes, it did die very soon, but it was already called the Action Party back then.

Silvio Ortona?

Silvio Ortona went on being a Communist and he still is. All the others were in the Action Party.

But did you talk about politics or not, or just a little?

You see, the situation had erupted with Badoglio and lasted a very short time, it lasted for forty-five days which we spent in the way you would least expect, that is to say all of us going on holiday to Cogne, heedless of what was about to happen and what it was obvious would happen, but we told ourselves that there were Italian divisions at the Brenner Pass which would form a barricade and that the Germans wouldn't arrive. And we believed that and we made some fairly reckless excursions in Cogne, during one of which Silvio Ortona fell and broke his front teeth. He fell fifteen metres.

A serious accident.

A serious accident, he was saved by a miracle, he was saved by a rock ledge.

It still seems incredible to me that you could believe in something so incredible.

It was typical. But of the whole of Italy, not just of us. The whole of Italy was in that state of mind. The 25th of July had been a great celebration and even on the 8th of September, the day of the armistice, everyone went down into the public squares to shout 'hurrah' for a day.

And you spent the whole of that period like that.

The forty-five days of Badoglio in the most happy-go-lucky way, but not only us. All the *kurort*[95] of Italy were full, in spite of the war, in spite of the threat which – with hind-sight – was both obvious and imminent.

You told me once that that period in Milan was also a time when you read a lot.

Yes, although if I had to tell you what I read at that time I wouldn't be able to remember. Perhaps I read *Budden-brooks*,[96] but I don't really remember. And then it's not as if we spent all that much time reading. We were involved in that complicated friendship.

At any rate, that was when you started writing, apart from those two stories which you had written earlier and which you included in The Periodic Table. *Stories that, if I'm not mistaken, date back to the period in Balangero.*

Yes ... Listen, though, here I have a confession to make.

---

[95] A German word meaning a spa, a health resort. (GT)
[96] *Buddenbrooks*, published in 1901 and based on the history of his own family, was Thomas Mann's first novel.

Do you want to record it or shall I switch this off?

As you like ... That is a falsehood, it's not true that I wrote those stories ...

What do you mean?

I wrote them later, but it struck me as a good idea to attribute them to that period.

I don't think that matters. It seems to me a legitimate use of fiction. And then the style of the writing leads us to believe in an awkwardness, a lack of experience.

Which was simulated.

Precisely. In literature it is legitimate to pass off a simulation as the truth.

That's what I did, I passed them off, I backdated those two stories. And I also wrote that poem, 'Crescenzago', which is typically childish.

Did you really write that during your time in Milan?

Yes, that's really true.

Well now, only answer this if you want to. Why do you feel that the exposure of something you consider to be a falsehood is so discreditable?

By analogy. Because I told it to everybody and wrote it down as well.

But isn't that the result of a very dominant super-ego?[97]

Possibly. At any rate, I didn't write those two stories in conjunction with *The Periodic Table*, I wrote them separately and then included them under the titles 'Mercury' and 'Lead'.

During your time in Milan did you only write 'Crescenzago', or anything else as well?

Yes, I didn't write any other poems.

And you didn't have any other writing projects in mind?

The one that I told you about, that unfinished story which was started and never completed, never developed.

Were your friends trying their hands at it too?

That is the case, my friends were writing too. Silvio Ortona was writing a philosophical treatise, Eugenio Gentili was writing a so-called anti-novel, my cousin Ada Della Torre, I didn't tell you her name earlier ...

You already told me her name when I was writing my critical portrait of you for Belfagor...[98]

Yes, she wrote poetry and worked for the publisher Dall'Oglio.[99] So I was really immersed in a

[97] In Freudian psychoanalytic theory, the super-ego, the part of the personality which reflects the moral and cultural rules acquired in childhood, acts as a kind of strict internal critic in adult life.
[98] *Belfagor*: see n. 13 on p. xv.
[99] Enrico Dall'Oglio (1900–1966) founded the left-wing publishing house, Corbaccio, later called Corbaccio-Dall'Oglio, in 1923.

literary environment and I felt it was obligatory to write something.

So it wasn't an inner drive, a personal compulsion.

No, it was through imitation.

But also because you had already had the idea of writing. Did you never try to write while you were at the liceo, *did you never make the attempt?*

No, never.

This period you've been telling me about, how long did it last? You were in Balangero until June '42?

Yes, and in Milan until the catastrophe, until the 8th of September '43.

And on the 8th of September were you in Cogne?

No, no, I was already back in Milan.

What was the working environment like at Wander?

I can't add much to what I wrote in the 'Phosphorus' chapter, indeed I feel that I have already said enough about it. It was a very sterile environment. There was that dear friend that I still have and who is – though I didn't write about it – seriously disabled, she always has been, she was born like that, but she has lived a full life all the same.

Despite the state censorship which necessitated a certain amount of compromise, Corbaccio remained an anti-fascist as well as a literary firm, and Dall'Oglio himself was forced into exile in Switzerland in 1944.

Is that also why you are so involved with that girl who lives in an iron lung, what is she called?

Rosanna Benzi?[100] No, it was she who contacted me. Hers is a really unique case.

You say that this lasted until the 8th of September. And then?

Right away, in fact as soon as the Germans reached Milan, on the 10th of September I think, I came back here to where my family had taken refuge near Superga.[101] My grandfather owned a farm, it had been part of a monastery, and the whole of my extended family were encamped there. My mother, my sister and I met there and we thought about what we should do and we decided to go to the Val d'Aosta, where there were some people we knew, and from the Val d'Aosta – from Saint-Vincent – we were advised to

[100] Rosanna Benzi (1948–1991), who was struck down, when she was not yet fourteen, by bulbospinal poliomyelitis [a paralytic form of the disease affecting the medulla: the part of the brain which controls swallowing, breathing and speech], was forced by her illness to live her life in an iron lung. All the same, she managed to work tirelessly on behalf of the disabled, including confronting thorny questions such as their sexuality, through the journal *Gli Altri* [The Others] which she founded, and through her books, some of which, such as *Il vizio di vivere* [The Vice of Living] (1984) and *Girotondo in una stanza* [A Ring-of-Roses in My Room] (1987), received considerable acclaim. Primo Levi wrote to her and talked about this in *La Stampa*. (GT)

A letter from Levi to Rosanna Benzi, 'That train to Auschwitz', is included in Primo Levi and Leonardo De Benedetti, *Auschwitz Testimonies: 1945–1986*, op. cit., pp. 148–151.

[101] La Saccarella, the country villa of Levi's maternal grandfather Cesare Luzzati, is on a hill near the Basilica of Superga, the mausoleum where members of the royal House of Savoy were traditionally interred.

go to a remote inn in the Col de Joux, which is still there, but now there is also a road which goes all the way there, back then there was no road, you had to make your way 1,000 metres higher up the hill, and we moved into that inn, my mother, my sister and I, to await events. And then soldiers started to arrive from all directions. Among them there was one who was almost a classmate of mine, he was a year younger than me.

At the D'Azeglio or at university?

At the D'Azeglio. We ignored each other for a little while and then the charade of not recognizing each other began to feel stupid and that gave rise to the idea of declaring ourselves to be partisans, but it was all so precarious, so rough and ready, so rudimentary, we had no contacts. We had the idea that we ought to do something, take up arms, but we didn't have any arms. We made some contacts and we gathered around ourselves a group of a dozen young men, as ill-prepared as ourselves. There was only one who had had some military experience.

What kind of young men?

Ones who should have presented themselves for military service and hadn't done so, one of them was Jewish.

And where did you find them?

They arrived of their own accord, they came up to the inn, they came from those parts and were looking for a refuge.

What was the place called?

It was called Amay. It isn't a hotel, it's a group of five houses.

Does it still exist and have you been back there?

Yes.

So you were talking about young men who came up there in search of a solution.

And they too had hazy ideas about arming themselves and resisting. Some of them had revolvers, we even got hold of a submachine gun, I don't remember who brought it. It was all extremely hazy.

But, however nebulously, you wanted to form yourselves into a small partisan band.

Yes.

And did you look for contacts to enable you to join up with one?

Yes indeed, we looked for them and we found them. Then it so happened that in the next valley, the Val d'Ayas, there was a large and established band which had attacked the barracks in Ivrea, taking prisoners and also killing someone, I think, and it resulted in a large-scale reprisal. Three hundred soldiers came from Ivrea in a pincer movement. They came right up to Saint-Vincent and found us as well.

They found you completely defenceless?

Absolutely defenceless.

Was it by day or at night?

It was at dawn.

Were you in bed?

We were in bed.

And then what happened?

What happened was that some of us were captured. Some were alerted in time and managed to escape. I was in bed, I had a revolver which they didn't find. They took me to Aosta and in Aosta they interrogated me about what I was doing there, what had I gone there to do, and I told them I was Jewish. I stupidly told them that.

What made you say that?

It is hard to reconstruct. Partly because I had fake identity papers, so fake that ...

You couldn't hold out?

And then it was they themselves – the Fascists, not the Germans – who said, 'If you are a partisan, we will shoot you, but if you are a Jew we'll send you to Carpi[102] where there is an internment camp and you will stay there until the end of the war'. And then there was my stupidity, my blindness, but as I told you, the wisdom of hindsight ... I believed that the Salò administration was a stable one, without German interference ... Foreseeing the future ... And then there was also a kind of pride.

---

[102] The Fossoli di Carpi internment camp for Italian and foreign Jews, near the city of Modena, eventually became a deportation camp from which nearly three thousand men, women and children were transported to Auschwitz.

That is just what I wanted to ask you. Did a certain sense of belonging also come into it?

We too, if the need arises, know how to, and want to stand up for ourselves. Besides, I would have had to invent an army division that I belonged to and I didn't know how to do that. I was of military age, I was in a military setting, so why wasn't I doing military service? There was a reason.

Why didn't you do military service?

Because of the racial laws.

How long were you held prisoner in Aosta?

From the 13th of December, when I was captured, until my deportation, which you will find in my books. I think it was the 22nd of February.

In Aosta the whole time?

No, no, I was in Aosta for about a month, in the barracks, in the prison cellars.

It must have been very cold.

Yes, it was cold.

Were you reasonably treated?

It was a prison regime, they gave us soup at midday and in the evening, an hour of open-air exercise, a bucket.

One to a cell or all together?

We were together for a few days to begin with, then they separated us.

You were in solitary confinement?

Solitary, yes.

Do you think that they did that to prevent you from communicating?

Yes, that's the explanation.

And then, after a month, you were transported to Fossoli? How did you get there?

By train. I tried to bribe a military policeman. We had been handed over to the military police for the journey, I tried to bribe one of them but I didn't succeed.

He refused you point-blank?

Well, he hesitated, then he said no, he didn't trust me.

What were relations like with the guards in the camp?

I would say that they were quite decent, they turned a blind eye to a lot of things, they even accompanied some of us who needed treatment to the dentist in Modena. It was a decent regime and everyone allowed themselves to think that it would actually continue like that until the end of the war. Instead, a little while before our deportation, that is to say in mid February, the SS arrived and ousted the Italians from the running of the camp and, a few days later, they put us on a train.

How was the camp organized from a logistical point of view?

It's still there. There were brick huts, fairly clean, with a central kitchen. The weather was good.

Was it very large?

No, no, it was about half a square kilometre, it used to be a camp for English prisoners of war.

And what chores did you have? Did you do any or not?

No.

Did the running arrangements depend on volunteers? For the cleaning and the cooking?

Yes, there were volunteers for the cooking and the cleaning. I did a bit of cleaning if I'm not mistaken.

And the rest of the time?

Nothing.

Literally nothing? Weren't there even any books being passed around?

Yes ... No, I was forgetting that I did some teaching, I taught Italian, Latin and mathematics to the children.

Did you do that throughout your time there? Were you running a sort of school?

A little school.

Were there more than one of you doing that, or did you do it on your own?

There were two or three of us.

Did you organize the teaching yourselves to make up for the lack of education?

Yes. All of it, of course, under the illusion that things would go on like that.

What about books and exercise books, did you have to make do as best you could or was it possible to get hold of some?

They could be ordered, it could be done straight from the prison camp, they could be ordered in Modena.

Did anyone manage to set up a support system for escape attempts?

Nobody escaped from Fossoli. We thought that there was no need, and then all of us were bourgeois. It would have required a great sense of adventure but I don't think it would have been impossible to escape. We were all, or nearly all, there with our families. Escaping on one's own, leaving friends or family members behind, seemed something ... But I have to count it among my many mistakes, not having tried to escape.

Where would you have gone?

That wouldn't really have been a great problem. Once outside, one could have gone to Modena, gone to a priest, looked for a contact.

Speaking of personal relationships, did you get to know anyone in Fossoli?

Some very pleasant, very courageous and very clear-sighted Croatian Jews who told us, 'We're not going to get out of here'.

You have never said much about Fossoli in your writing.

I have qualms ... I have qualms ...

You've said far more about the Lager than you have about Fossoli.

Yes indeed, I have qualms. And also about that woman I told you of.

Now let's make a quantum leap forward. Let's try talking about the time after the Lager, let's try going back to the subject of employment, of your work.

Afterwards I found work quite quickly with Montecatini, with Duco in Avigliana which belonged to Montecatini.[103] And it was disagreeable. It was a big, dilapidated building, full of draughts, where nobody paid any attention to me, until the episode I described in 'Chromium'.[104]

What position did you have there?

I was a laboratory chemist.

You've talked about that, you used to take the train ...

Yes, sometimes I used to cycle there. While I was in Avigliana I got engaged.

---

[103] The paint factory DUCO (Du Pont de Nemours and Co.), a subsidiary of the large mining, chemicals and explosives company Nobel-Montecatini, was situated in Avigliana, a lakeside village northeast of Turin.
[104] In 'Chromium', Levi describes the detective work which enabled him to discover why a batch of orange paint had coagulated into a

And that was the best thing about this period. But how long did you stay at Duco?

From February '46 to June '47.

And what made you leave?

What made me leave? Folly, that is to say a fresh proposal from Alberto Salmoni that we should get back together. That was another mistake. I can't say that it was a mistake, because if I had stayed at Duco I would have been transferred to Codogno, I would have spent an entire wretched career with Montecatini, with Montedison,[105] I would have had to settle in Codogno and I wouldn't have accepted that position with Siva,[106] which was providential.

It's always hard to evaluate an error of judgement.

That's how it turned out.

'gelatinous and softish mass' (*The Periodic Table*, op. cit., p. 152), a problem with which he became so enamoured that his new fiancée was actually 'a little jealous of it' (p. 156). Although it is a comic story, it also contains the tragic memory of Vanda Maestro and Levi's euphoria at finally falling in love.

[105] The troubled history of the Montecatini company led to a merger with Edison in 1966, but serious problems continued throughout the entire period of Levi's career and beyond, so his rash decision to leave DUCO in 1948 was in fact a lucky escape, even apart from the fact that it saved him from having to leave his home in Turin and move to Codogno in Lombardy.

[106] When Levi joined it in 1948, Siva, the Società Industriale Vernici e Affini [Industrial Paints and Related Products Company], was a small paint factory on the outskirts of Turin. During Levi's time there, and partly due to his work, it expanded into a successful firm specializing in insulation paint for electric wires.

Did your new enterprise with Salmoni start a little more successfully than the previous one?

A little more successfully, yes, we earned a bit, we got something done.

And where were your premises this time?

At 43 Via Massena ... no, it was an even number, it was 42.

How many rooms? An apartment?

One room and a balcony, plus an invasion into other rooms if necessary.

And what about the apparatus? Did you go half and half? Did you pay your share?

No, I had nothing, I was on an allowance. Alberto Salmoni set it all up and the allowance wasn't sufficient for me, so when I had the offer to join Siva I accepted it right away.

I thought you had set up the business as partners?

I had no money.

And what did he do afterwards? Did he close down?

Yes, he gave up too. He kept going for a few months longer and then he found himself a job as well.

Who offered you the job at Siva?

The father of a friend of mine, the engineer Livio Norzi, acted as an intermediary with Siva, as he was a friend of the owner.

The owner of Siva is ...

Federico Accati, who was looking for a young chemist and employed me right away.

Did you become a manager right away?

No, I started at the bottom of the ladder: laboratory chemist.

And when did this happen?

It happened in '47, no, in February '48.

So you started travelling to Settimo ...[107]

No, at that time Siva was in Turin, it was in Corso Regina.

How far up?

Near to the shooting range, at the west end, at the Martinetto. Siva stayed there until '55, then it moved to Settimo and I moved with it.

Had you already been promoted by that point?

I was already the technical manager, my predecessor had died.

---

[107] Settimo Torinese is a suburb seven miles from Turin.

What was he called?

Osvaldo Gianotti, he was an old chemical expert. He was as old as I am now, he seemed very old to me.

So you became technical manager. What's the difference between a technical manager and – I suppose – an administrative one?

Well, there is also the general manager. Being technical manager means being responsible for production in a practical sense.

Which year did you become general manager?

In '61.

And you stayed there until you retired?

I retired in '75 and I stayed on for another two years as a consultant.

When the factory moved to Settimo in '55, how did you get there? There is a poem, 'Via Cigna', which talks about that.[108]

I always went by car, I never once used public transport.

What kind of car did you have? I mean your first car …

My first car was a Fiat Giardinetta, then I had an Appia, then I had a Fulvia, then I had an Autobianchi.

---

[108] *Collected Poems*, op. cit., p. 28. Levi's poem, written in 1973, describes the seemingly endless misery of driving as a commuter down a dismal street in the dark.

Not many cylinders, then.

No, the Fulvia had the most.

A life spent in the factory.

Thirty years, from '47 to '77.

They were the central years of your adult life. What memories do you have of them? You've already told a part of that in your stories, but could you give an idea of a typical day?

I would arrive and go round all the departments to see if everything was running smoothly ...

Excuse the interruption, but have you always been an early riser?

Yes.

You don't mind getting up?

It's a habit being an early riser. I had to be there, in Settimo, by eight.

So your working day began at eight.

I would go round the departments and hear what had happened during the night, because the work was in shifts, including night shifts, then I would read the mail and answer it, I would meet with representatives. I would eat in the factory, there was a canteen. Various things, problems of all kinds. I would often spend the day in the laboratory, because I never gave up the laboratory, to formulate new kinds of varnish.

Do you have a tendency to rely on the work of others?

I didn't rely much on the work of others, at least in the early days. Then, in '65, we took on another chemist who was younger than me and thus more up to date than me and I delegated a lot of things to him. In the meantime I had made a great many journeys, initially by car with the boss who was fanatical about multi-cylinder cars.

Did you feel a little nervous?

No, no, he was a very good driver. Most of our journeys were to Germany, but also to Spain, and we even found ourselves in Norway, all by car, where I acted as interpreter and secretary so I had to speak German and English. Those are quite pleasant memories. The boss, with whom I had a purely formal working relationship in the factory, became extremely sociable, friendly and pleasant when we were travelling, and even accommodating, so much so that sometimes he allowed me a detour to go and talk, for example, in Frankfurt, with the publisher of *If This is a Man*.

And he appreciated your work as a writer?

Yes, but in silence, he didn't talk about it much.

Also because perhaps it might have embarrassed you?

He instinctively kept the two things separate: you are a chemist so get on with doing chemistry in my time, that's what I'm paying you for.

So when you got back, your normal relationship resumed.

Yes.

Not any more amicable.

Not really.

Did you make your journeys to the USSR with him?

In the final stages I also made a number of journeys on my own, both to Germany and to Russia. I went with a secretary-interpreter who was also a friend of mine. She was very good at establishing diplomatic relations, so to speak, with the Russians.

Germany, England, Norway, the USSR ...

To Germany many times, at least twenty, to England three or four times, once to Spain, once to Norway, three times to Russia, once to Austria.

How was it the first time in Germany?

It was in '51 if I'm not mistaken.

But did it make a particular impression on you?

Yes, yes, it made a particular impression on me. There were still mounds of rubble and I went there unwillingly, I felt that it was wrong and that I ought not to be doing business with the Germans.

Let's stay with the factory for a moment. Memorable characters?

I had a real friendship with the 'bo'sun', the foreman of the factory, who was a lad from Verolengo. A fine person: brave, intelligent, helpful, good at handling the workers, who spoke in dialect and who died tragically, falling from scaffolding, not in the factory.

Was he your inspiration for the character of Faussone?[109]

No.

So who was your inspiration for that character?

He originated with the various mechanics I had dealings with, particularly the mechanics of a sister factory to ours, belonging to the same proprietor, which still exists – it's called Sicme and is in Via Cigna in Turin – and assembles equipment for coating copper wire, and it was from talking to the mechanics there that the idea of Faussone was born.

As manager did you deal directly with the workers or were there intermediaries?

I dealt directly with some of them, who were my own team, and through that 'bo'sun' with the others.

Do you have what in military life they call leadership qualities?

I've never been very good at that sort of thing, I used to delegate the giving of orders to that factory foreman.

[109] The hero of Levi's novel, *The Wrench*.

Traumatic incidents that you recall? I mean human inci-
dents that caused difficulties for you?

It's rather hard to remember. Workers with serious family
problems, one who stole ...

From the factory?

Yes.

Did you have difficulty in dealing with that?

Yes, I had to sack him. I often overlooked the fact that I
had found somebody smoking. Smoking was forbidden,
sometimes I turned a blind eye.

How many workers were there?

Up to a maximum of seventy, but to start with, still in
Corso Regina, there were seven.

Is it still a successful factory?

The factory has halved in size now, but what's left of it is
quite successful and there is still equipment there designed
by me.

When you had problems at the factory, did you have a
tendency to take them home with you?

Yes.

You didn't manage to switch off ...

No. Then they used to telephone me, I don't know, sometimes even at night. I had to go there more than once,
two or three times, at night, to see to something, to
sort something out. I remember when my son was born
in '57. My son was born at four in the morning, but
by seven I was already in Settimo because a hail storm
had caused I don't know what kind of damage. I was
conscientious.

*I don't doubt it. But in all those years in the factory did
you never think about making a change, doing something
else? Setting up your own company, for instance?*

Setting up my own company, no, not after the experiences
I've had. Out of the question. I don't have what it takes to
be an industrialist. I longed for retirement, I'd had enough,
especially of those night-time calls. Have I already told you
about that accident?

*The fire you thought you were putting out by throwing
inflammable material onto it? But then there was also this
separate life that you led.*

I ask myself how I found the energy to do all that, it's a
mystery.

I ask myself that too.

Yet I wrote the whole of *The Truce* between '61 and '62.

*Did you write in the factory too, if you had any spare
time?*

I always wrote at home, I used to write after dinner, I
found the will and the strength.

Quite astonishing, in fact.

I wrote *The Periodic Table* when I knew I was going to retire. I couldn't have done it before, I couldn't have talked about the factory, I had an inhibition about it.